Robert Hammer

The Revival of the Organ Case

THE·REVIVAL·OF
THE·ORGAN·CASE

JOSEPH · EDWIN · BLANTON

Venture Press · 1965 · Albany Texas

TO MY UNCLE
JOE B. MATTHEWS
FOR WHOM I WAS NAMED

ACKNOWLEDGEMENTS

It would be impossible to gather together a collection of photographs like this and the data contained in the captions without the co-operation of a great number of people. Those who supplied the published photographs are listed below. Others sent photographs which for one reason or another could not be included but I am no less grateful to those persons for their willingness to help. When the firm of Walcker of Ludwigsburg could not send requested photographs of their organs in the Matthäuskirche in Berlin-Steglitz and St. Antonius in Essen-Frohnhausen, they offered me their printing plates but for technical reasons these could not be used. Even if I had made notes of the names of all the people who have helped me during the research for this little volume, I could not begin to list them. There have been organists and other church staff members who have replied to written queries and many others who extended courtesies when I visited their churches. I think of numbers of individuals such as the kindly gentleman in Aabenraa who acted as my interpreter there and the good women who were scrubbing the great church in Sorö who unlocked the door for me. The greatest in number have been the principals and employees of the organ-building firms whose help was essential to this work. I am also grateful for the confidence and patience of the subscribers. For their part in the actual book production, I must thank my aunt, Mrs. H. H. Brittingham, and my sister, Miss Anne Blanton, for providing work space; George L. Bozeman, Jr., for reading proofs; and Messrs. A. O. Evans, Byron Gore, Tye Callaway, Jr., Roy Anderson and H. V. Chapman Jr., for invaluable co-operation in working out details of manufacture.

CREDITS FOR PHOTOGRAPHS

Names of photographers who supplied photographs appear at the margin; otherwise, names of photographers, when known, follow names of suppliers. Key to letters after page numbers:— R: right; C: center; L: left; T: top; B: bottom

Supplied by Aeolian-Skinner Organ Co., Inc., Boston, Mass. 75L.

Supplied by Andover Organ Co., Inc., Methuen, Mass. Hughes Co. 88.

Supplied by Rudolf von Beckerath, Hamburg, Germany 64L; Wehmeier 73; Gottfried Jäger 74L.

Author 38L, 44L, 44R, 45L, 45R, 49, 56R, 57L, 62, 66L, 90L, 90R, 91L, 91R, 96TL, 96TR.

George L. Bozeman, Jr. 39L, 86L.

Supplied by Ted Brooks, Sulphur, La. 79B.

Supplied by Casavant Frères Limitée, Ste. Hyacinthe, P.Q., Canada. R. Bélanger 33; Studio Lumiere 35R; Hellmuth Wolff 63; Studio Fotomi 65L, 65R; R. B. Mccaulay 94T; Karl Wilhelm 94B.

Supplied by Delaware Organ Co., Inc., Tonawanda, N.Y. John R. Kennedy 37R; Phil Brodatz 39R.

Cleveland Fisher 74R.

Supplied by D. A. Flentrop, Zaandam, Netherlands 40L, 40R, 41L, 41R, 46R, 59TL, 59TR, 61L, 76.

Supplied by Th. Frobenius & Co., Lyngby, Copenhagen, Denmark 47R, 78, 79T.

Supplied by Gress-Miles Organ Co., Inc., Pennington, N.J. Joseph Frischman 36L, 36R; David Falconer 36C.

Supplied by Nils Hammarberg, Olof Hammarberg Orgelbyggare, Gothenburg, Sweden 67L, 69R; Björn Rodhe 67R; Richard Graber 68L; Kjell Gustavsson 68R; Karl G. Svensson 69L, 92T; Lundby Foto 86R; Bertil Reijbrandt 87R, Leif Wirén 95T.

Supplied by Hill, Norman & Beard Ltd., London, England 37L; C. H. Wood Ltd. 77.

Supplied by Otto Hofmann, Austin, Tex. Margret Hofmann 34R.

Supplied by Johannes Klais Orgelbau KG, Bonn, Germany 95B; Hans Gerd Klais 35L, 43, 47L, 52, 58TL, 58TR, 58BL, 58BR, 59BL, 59BR, 60L, 60C, 60R, 75R, 80L, 80R, 81L, 81R, 82, 83R, 84L, 84R, 85L, 85R, 92B, 93T.

Supplied by Orgelbau Th. Kuhn AG, Männedorf, Switzerland 34L, 46L, 87L, 96BL.

Supplied by Ernst Leeflang, Apeldoorn, Netherlands. H. Stokhuyzen 50; Publicam 51.

Supplied by Marcussen & Sön, Aabenraa, Denmark 70R; S. J. Zachariassen 53, 66R; A. Wendig 55; J. F. van Os 56L; K. Jensen 57R; 70L; Jonals & Co. 71L, 71R.

Supplied by Rieger Orgelbau, Schwarzach, Vorarlberg, Austria. Schmölz & Ullrich 83L.

Supplied by the Rector, St. Joseph's Oratory, Montreal, P.Q., Canada 64R.

Supplied by Schantz Organ Co., Orrville, Ohio. Paul A. Kaufman 96BR.

Supplied by Schlicker Organ Co., Inc., Buffalo, N.Y. John D. Schiff 89

Supplied by Gerhard Schmid Orgelbau, Kaufbeuren, Germany. Alfred Mayer 37C; Walter Köster 61R, Paul Kutter 72; Hans Heidig 93B.

Supplied by Gebr. van Vulpen, Utrecht, Netherlands 42, 48, 54.

Supplied by Van Zoeren, Henderson & Steinkampf, New York, N.Y. 38R.

SUBSCRIBERS

Mr. Richard L. Abbott, Santa Monica, California
Mrs. Robert H. Adams, Sturgis, Michigan
The Agnes Scott College Library, Decatur, Georgia
Mr. Gerald P. Allen, Lumberton, North Carolina
Dr. Robert T. Anderson, Dallas, Texas
Mr. Charles H. Angelo, III, Philadelphia, Pennsylvania
Dr. David H. Archer, Pittsburgh, Pennsylvania
University of Arizona Library, Tucson, Arizona
General Library, University of Arkansas, Fayetteville, Arkansas
Mr. D. Byron Arneson, Alliance, Ohio
Mr. Robert E. Arnold, New York, New York
Mr. M. Gerald Arthur, Boulder, Colorado
Mr. Robert T. Atkins, Troy, North Carolina
Mr. Walter L. Baggett, Nashville, Tennessee
Mr. Douglas S. Baker, Andalusia, Alabama
Mr. Henry Karl Baker, Nashua, New Hampshire
Mr. Dene Barnard, Canton, Ohio
Mr. J. S. R. Baxter, Norwich, Norfolk, England
Mr. Henry K. Beard, Barrington, Illinois
Beardslee Library, Western Theological Seminary, Holland, Michigan
Mr. William L. Bearley, Covina, California
Mr. Bruce Bennet, Cambridge, Massachusetts
Mr. Edward H. Bennett, Jr., Chicago, Illinois
Mr. Robert C. Bettany, Steyning, Sussex, England
Mr. David J. Billeter, Altadena, California
Mr. Roland S. Blackburn, Jr., Brooklyn, New York
Mr. Lyle W. Blackinton, El Cajon, California
The Rev. Marvin H. Blake, Montebello, California
Miss Anne Blanton, Albany, Texas
Mr. and Mrs. John M. Blanton, Albany, Texas
Mr. and Mrs. Thomas L. Blanton, Jr., Albany, Texas
Mr and Mrs William W. Blanton, Odessa, Texas
Mr. E. A. Boadway, Methuen, Massachusetts
Mr. Willis Bodine, Gainesville, Florida
The Rev. Edward T. Bollinger, Denver, Colorado
Mr. Robert J. Bonnor, Tecumseh, Michigan
Dr. Eldon G. Bowman, Wooster, Ohio
Mr. George L. Bozeman, Jr., Dallas, Texas
Mr. F. H. Bradbeer, Hatfield, Hertfordshire, England
Mr. James M. Bratton, Denver, Colorado
Mr. Douglas R. Breitmayer, St. Louis, Missouri
Mrs. George S. Brewer, Erie, Pennsylvania
Mrs. H. H. Brittingham, Fort Worth, Texas
Mr. W. A. Brummer, Granite City, Illinois
Mr. Ivis H. Brummett, Little Rock, Arkansas
Mr. Robert Brune, Dallas, Texas
Mr. Nelson E. Buechner, Philadelphia, Pennsylvania
Mrs. A. P. Burns, Pauls Valley, Oklahoma
Mr. William G. Burt, Jr., Weston, Massachusetts
Mr. William S. Butler, Ludington, Michigan
Mr. Clifton Caldwell, Albany, Texas
Bente Memorial Library, California Concordia College, Oakland, California
Mr. Roy H. Carey, Jr., Carlsbad, New Mexico
Mr. Del W. Case, Monterey Park, California
Mrs. Ethel Matthews Casey, Albany, Texas
Mrs. Curtis A. Chapel, Seattle, Washington
Mr. Sidney R. Chase, Worcester, New York
Mr. John Chrastina, Kansas City, Missouri
Mr. G. G. Chrestensen, Midwest City, Oklahoma
Mr. Brooks Clement, Carmel, California
Cooley and Borre, Park Ridge, Illinois
Mr. William M. Cooley, Park Ridge, Illinois
Mr. Hubert Corina, Cleveland, Ohio
Mrs. Robert R. Covell, Newport, Rhode Island

The Rev. Leonard J. Cross, Michigan City, Indiana
Mr. Lewis Crutcher, Portland, Oregon
Mr. Richard Cummins, Roanoke, Virginia
Mr. Thomas W. Cunningham, Cincinnati, Ohio
Mr. Donald D. Curry, Lincroft, New Jersey
The Very Rev. Msgr. Richard B. Curtin, Yonkers, New York
Dr. Ivan E. Danhof, Grand Prairie, Texas
Mrs. C. P. Daniel, Bristol, Virginia
Baker Library, Dartmouth College, Hanover, New Hampshire
Mr. Clele D'Autrey, Portland, Oregon
Mr. Robert L. David, Gary, Indiana
Mr. Vernon Perdue Davis, Richmond, Virginia
Mr. William R. Davis, Bronxville, New York
Mr. Rodney Leslie Degner, Omaha, Nebraska
Mr. Harold De La Chapelle, Thomaston, Connecticut
Detroit Public Library, Detroit, Michigan
Mr. Richard D. Dinwiddie, Cleveland Heights, Ohio
Mr. R. W. Dirksen, Freeport, Illinois
Mr. Joe Doms, Muldoon, Texas
The Rev. James L. Doom, Atlanta, Georgia
Mr. Robert R. Douglas, Oakland, California
Mr. Charles P. Drake, New Bedford, Massachusetts
Mr. Frank C. Drews, Jr., Middle Village, New York
Mr. Antoine DuBourg, Elizabeth, New Jersey
The Theological Seminary Library, University of Dubuque, Dubuque, Iowa
Mr. Brantley A. Duddy, Philadelphia, Pennsylvania
Mr. Thomas S. Eader, Ellicott City, Maryland
Mr. Ramon G. Evans, Carthage, Missouri
Mr. Charles J. Farris, Chambersburg, Pennsylvania
Mr. David Fedder, St. Louis, Missouri
Miss Paula A. Fendler, Spokane, Washington
Mr. Cleveland Fisher, Manassas, Virginia
Music Department, Father Flanagan's Boys' Home, Boys Town, Nebraska
The University of Florida Libraries, Gainesville, Florida
Mr. Wallace Curtis Flower, Erie, Pennsylvania
Mr. Robert L. Foley, Wichita, Kansas
Mr. Rubin S. Freis, Victoria, Texas
Mr. Charles G. Frischmann, Cranford, New Jersey
Mr. Wayne Froelich, New Braunfels, Texas
Mr. Carl S. Fudge, Jr., Elizabeth, New Jersey
Mr. Edward B. Gammons, Groton, Massachusetts
Mr. Hugo Gehrke, Oakland, California
Mr. Glenn A. Gentry, Jackson, Mississippi
Mr. Pierce Getz, Annville, Pennsylvania
Mr. Glenn Giffin, II, Boulder, Colorado
Mr. Michael Gillingham, London, England
Mr. Ben Gipson, Evanston, Illinois
Mr. Philip E. Glass, State College, Pennsylvania
Savitz Library, Glassboro State College, Glassboro, New Jersey
Mr. Robert W. Glover, Chico, California
Mr. Antone Godding, Waterbury, Connecticut
Charles M. Goodman Associates, Washington, District of Columbia
Mr. Larry Gorjup, Cleveland, Ohio
Mr. Don P. Gorman, Spokane, Washington
Mr. John T. Gotjen, Warren, Rhode Island
Mr. Frank R. Green, Lawrence, Kansas
Mr. Paul E. Green, Jr., Weston, Massachusetts
Mr. Milton L. Grigg, Charlottesville, Virginia
Mr. Conrad Grimes, Winnipeg, Manitoba, Canada
Mrs. Fred Grimes, Jr., Hillsboro, Texas

7

Mr. Harry E. Gudmundson, Whitmore Lake, Michigan
Mr. Andre Guilbault, La Providence, Ste. Hyacinthe, Quebec, Canada
Mr. Paul W. Gunzelmann, Princeton, New Jersey
Mr. Luther Gutknecht, Grand Rapids, Michigan
Mr. David L. Haar, Lincoln, Nebraska
Miss Ila Marie Hajek, Chicago, Illinois
Mr. Robert K. Hale, Gossville, New Hampshire
Mrs. Richard J. Halford, Houston, Texas
Mr. William C. Hall, San Antonio, Texas
Mr. H. Theodore Hallman, Jr., Souderton, Pennsylvania
Mr. Donald L. Hand, Hartford, Connecticut
Mr. Rodney Hansen, Stamford, Connecticut
Mr. Milton D. Harmelink, Downsview, Ontario, Canada
Mr. Raymond Harris, Macon, Georgia
Mr. John W. Harvey, Madison, Wisconsin
Mr. Walter Hawkes, Merrimac, Massachusetts
Mr. Will O. Headlee, Syracuse, New York
Mr. Stephen G. Heaver, Jr., Baltimore, Maryland
Mr. Edgar B. Heflin, Jr., Alexandria, Virginia
Mr. Guy Frederick Henderson, Brooklyn, New York
Mr. Keith Paul Henderson, Dallas, Texas
Dr. Frank Herand, Honolulu, Hawaii
Mr. Victor Hildner, River Forest, Illinois
Mr. Richard Hillman, Michigan City, Indiana
Mrs. S. E. Hittson, Cisco, Texas
Mr. John T. Hofmann, Eggertsville, New York
Mr. Otto Hofmann, Austin, Texas
Mr. Roy H. Holmgren, San Mateo, California
Mr. E. A. Houlden, Westcliff-On-Sea, Essex, England
Mr. Timothy Housel, Pennington, New Jersey
Houston Baptist College, Houston, Texas
Mrs. Hubert A. Howell, Dixon, Illinois
Mr. Arthur Howes, Baltimore, Maryland
Mr. Donald G. Hoyer, Lawrence, Kansas
Dr. James F. Hyde, Jr., Ripon, Wisconsin
Mr. Kary W. Hyre, Seattle, Washington
Mr. Paul Curtis Irwin, Detroit, Michigan
Mr. Robert E. Ives, Huntsville, Alabama
The Rev. Thomas E. Jackson, Houston, Texas
Miss Joanne E. Jansen, Grand Rapids, Michigan
Mrs. Emil H. Jebe, Ann Arbor, Michigan
Mr. Oscar H. Jekel, Kirkwood, Missouri
Mr. Carl E. Johnson, Jr., Leavenworth, Kansas
Mr. Clarence Jones, Mt. Vernon, New York
Mr. and Mrs. Ardon B. Judd, Houston, Texas
Dr. Curtis W. V. Junker, Tulsa, Oklahoma
Mr. G. Herald Keefer, Vancouver, British Columbia, Canada
Mr. Roy F. Kehl, Kenmore, New York
Mr. D. Stuart Kennedy, Calgary, Alberta, Canada
Mr. Colin C. Kerr, Montreal, Quebec, Canada
Mr. Donald King, Baltimore, Maryland
Mr. Bertram Y. Kinzey, Jr., Gainesville, Florida
Mr. A. J. Kistler, Charlotte, North Carolina
Dr. John L. Klein, Muscatine, Iowa
Mr. William B. Knaus, Skokie, Illinois
Mr. Justin Kramer, Los Angeles, California
Dr. Adalbert R. Kretzmann, Chicago, Illinois
Mr. David K. Krohne, River Forest, Illinois
Mr. Frank L. Kuhlmann, Ann Arbor, Michigan
Mr. Terence C. Lake, Smethwick, Staffordshire, England
Mr. Richard Landes, Sacramento, California
Mr. Alan Laufman, Harrisville, New Hampshire

Mr. Peter Laukhuff, Weikersheim, Württemburg, Germany
Mr. James P. Lawbaugh, Colon, Nebraska
Mr. Arthur P. Lawrence, Berkeley, California
Mr. Edward H. Lawson, San Francisco, California
Mr. William S. Layne, Park Forest, Illinois
Mr. Max L. Leget, Vermillion, South Dakota
Mr. Edwin L. Lewis, Philadelphia, Pennsylvania
Mr. James H. Litton, Indianapolis, Indiana
Miss Margaret Litwiller, Rochester, New York
Dr. Robert Lodine, Chicago, Illinois
Mrs. L. H. Loomis, Concord, Massachusetts
Mr. Lewis H. Loomis, Parral, Chihuahua, Mexico
Mr. Gary Loper, Dallas, Texas
Mrs. Joseph A. Loris, Mansfield, Ohio
The School of Music Library, University of Louisville, Louisville, Kentucky
Mr. Alfred E. Lunsford, Knoxville, Tennessee
Mr. A. C. M. Luteijn, Bloemendaal, Netherlands
Miss Lorna K. Lutz, Williamson, New York
Mr. Michael B. McBride, Fort Collins, Colorado
Dr. Roy O. McClain, Atlanta, Georgia
Mr. Thomas L. McCook, Jr., Atlanta, Georgia
Mrs. Katheryn McCord, Chicago, Illinois
Mr. James B. McGregor, Newark, New Jersey
Mr. Charles W. McManis, Kansas City, Kansas
McMurry College Library, Abilene, Texas
Mr. Raymond Mabry, Richmond, Virginia
Mrs. Frank M. Madson, Orlando, Florida
Mr. Walter Robert Mahns, Oakhurst, New Jersey
Mr. Kenneth Ramsey Mason, Jamestown, Pennsylvania
Mr. and Mrs. Joe B. Matthews, Albany, Texas
Mr. Watt R. Matthews, Albany, Texas
Mr. Edwin H. May, Knoxville, Tennessee
The Rev. Earl L. Mayo, Malone, New York
Mr. John G. Meem, Santa Fe, New Mexico
Miami University Library, Oxford, Ohio
Mr. Joseph E. Michaud, Mt. Lebanon, Pennsylvania
Mr. Bradley F. Millard, Tacoma, Washington
Mr. Robert R. Miller, Dallas, Texas
Mr. Frederick L. Mitchell, West Hartford, Connecticut
Mr. Karl B. Mohr, Tallahassee, Florida
Dr. James M. Monaghan, Short Hills, New Jersey
Library of the Moravian College, Bethlehem, Pennsylvania
Mr. Louis G. Monette, Charlotte, North Carolina
Mr. Kenneth T. Morse, Dobbs Ferry, New York
Mr. Carl Natelli, Seattle, Washington
Mr. Richard H. Nealon, Delhi, New York
Mr. J. Paul Neary, Inglewood, California
Mr. Bruce W. Nehring, Dallas, Texas
Mr. Charles L. Neill, Upper Montclair, New Jersey
Mr. John D. Newall, Dallas, Texas
Mr. Raymond J. Newman, Ann Arbor, Michigan
Mr. Edwin D. Northrup, Cleveland, Ohio
Mr. Eugene M. Nye, Seattle, Washington
The Ohio State University Library, Columbus, Ohio
The Rev. C. H. Osborn, Portland, Oregon
Mr. Richard S. Oslund, Seattle, Washington
Mr. Thad H. H. Outerbridge, North Wilbraham, Massachusetts
Miss Barbara J. Owen, Pigeon Cove, Massachusetts
Dr. Edith Trugly Owen, Ladue, Missouri
Mr. Max Y. Parker, Kingsport, Tennessee
Mr. Robert O. Parrett, Lakeland, Florida
Mr. Richard Parsons, III, Raleigh, North Carolina

Mr. Franklin E. Perkins, St. Louis, Missouri
Mr. John E. Pfeil, Lynchburg, Virginia
The Free Library of Philadelphia, Philadelphia, Pennsylvania
Mr. Daniel F. Pilzecker, Toledo, Ohio
Mr. Keith E. E. Pittman, Pittsburgh, Pennsylvania
Mr. Robert B. Po-Chedley, Tonawanda, New York
Mr. William F. Pohl, Minneapolis, Minnesota
Mr. Thomas V. Potter, Hingham, Massachusetts
Mr. Joseph Prucnal, Johnstown, Pennsylvania
Mr. Phillip Puente, Dallas, Texas
Mr. J. David Rasche, Waukegan, Illinois
Mr. Ferd T. E. Rassman, Deal, New Jersey
Mr. E. C. Read, Saint John, New Brunswick, Canada
Mr. Donald S. Reed, Cranston, Rhode Island
Miss Myrtle Regier, South Hadley, Massachusetts
Mr. Leon G. Reimer, Baltimore, Maryland
Mr. John D. Reynolds, New York, New York
Mr. Ronald C. Rice, Takoma Park, Maryland
Mr. Roger A. Richard, Long Beach, California
Mr. Lowell Riley, Columbus, Ohio
Mr. Donald C. Rockwood, Norfolk, Massachusetts
Mills Memorial Library, Rollins College, Winter Park, Florida
Mr. Myles J. Rosenthal, New York, N.Y.
Mr. John M. Rossfeld, Detroit, Michigan
Mr. John M. Rucker, Walnut Creek, California
Mr. Wilbur F. Russell, San Anselmo, California
Mr. W. M. Rust, III, Houston, Texas
The St. Louis Public Library, St. Louis, Missouri
Mr. D. R. Salisbury, Pelham, New York
Mr. H. Wilton Samuelson, Sedro-Woolley, Washington
Mr. G. H. Sandin, Fortuna, California
Dr. Herbert B. Satcher, Philadelphia, Pennsylvania
Mr. Norman L. Scheck, Romeo, Michigan
The Rev. Alfred Schendel, Ehrenfeld, Pennsylvania
Dr. A. Benedict Schneider, Cleveland, Ohio
Mr. Josef Schnelker, Salem, Oregon
Mr. Daniel O. Schultz, Fishers, New York
Mr. James A. Schultz, Massapequa, New York
Mrs. Milford D. Schulz, Belmont, Massachusetts
Mr. Ed Schuricht, Inglewood, California
Mr. Benjamin B. Schwartz, Chicago, Illinois
Dr. John D. Seagrave, Los Alamos, New Mexico
Mr. J. T. Sears, Worcester, Worcestershire, England
Mr. Lee V. Seibert, Wyomissing, Pennsylvania
Mr. Ronald W. Sharp, Mortdale, New South Wales, Australia
Mr. Frank C. Shattuck, Neenah, Wisconsin
Mr. John F. Shawhan, Saginaw, Michigan
Mr. Olaf William Shelgren, Buffalo, New York
Mr. Raymond Shelley, Wichita, Kansas
Mr. George W. Shuppert, Parkton, Maryland
Mr. Jack L. Sievert, Lawrence, Kansas
Mr. Kenneth F. Simmons, Wayne, Pennsylvania
Mr. David Carter Sinclair, Clinton, New York
Mr. Robert L. Sipe, Dallas, Texas

Mr. Allan B. Sly, Squantum, Massachusetts
Mr. Emmet G. Smith, Fort Worth, Texas
Mr. Willard G. Smith, Los Angeles, California
Mr. James Dale Sonnier, Port Neches, Texas
Mr. Hugo Spilker, Victoria, British Columbia, Canada
Mr. Arthur C. Strahle, Flint, Michigan
Mr. Joseph A. Surace, New York, New York
Mr. Jon Atwood Swanson, Washington, District of Columbia
Mr. Paul F. Theilemann, Burnt Hills, New York
Mr. Glen C. Thomas, Wichita, Kansas
Mrs. J. E. Thomerson, St. Louis, Missouri
Mr. and Mrs. Robert B. Thrasher, Austin, Texas
The Toledo Museum of Art, Toledo, Ohio
The University of Toronto Library, Toronto, Ontario, Canada
Mr. Robert M. Turner, Hopewell, New Jersey
Summar Library, Union University, Jackson, Tennessee
Mr. Ralph B. Valentine, New York, New York
Mr. David J. Van Veghel, Minneapolis, Minnesota
Mr. Lloyd W. Vick, Mt. Gravatt, Queensland, Australia
Mr. Harold E. Wagoner, Philadelphia, Pennsylvania
Mr. David S. Walker, Douglaston, New York
Prof. David S. Walker, Flushing, New York
The Rev. George M. Walker, Albany, New York
Dr. Joseph Wallace, Jr., Lansdowne, Pennsylvania
Mr. William Wannemacher, St. Louis, Missouri
Mr. C. Edward Ware, Rockford, Illinois
The Washington Cathedral Library, Washington, District of Columbia
Dr. D. DeWitt Wasson, Dobbs Ferry, New York
Mr. Graham Watson, Bradford, Yorkshire, England
Mr. Harold W. Weaver, Columbus, Ohio
Mr. Malcolm Wechsler, Stamford, Connecticut
Mr. Harry A. Wells, Hickory, North Carolina
Mr. John West, San Francisco, California
Mr. Edward F. Whittaker Jr., Camden, New Jersey
Mr. Lawrence S. Whitten, Birmingham, Alabama
Mr. John T. Widener, Atlanta, Georgia
Mr. Julian J. Wilcox, Jr., Walton, New York
Mr. Thornton LaMoree Wilcox, Pittsburgh, Pennsylvania
Mr. Charles Wilhite, Fremont, Nebraska
Mr. Donald G. Wilkins, Pittsburgh, Pennsylvania
Mr. Dale Edward Willoughby, Miami, Florida
Mr. John Wilson, Kenmore, New York
The University of Wisconsin Memorial Library, Madison, Wisconsin
Mr. Jerry R. Witt, La Jolla, California
Mr. Barclay Wood, Worcester, Massachusetts
Mr. John W. Wood, Dallas, Texas
Mr. Robert L. Wyant, Arlington, Virginia
Mr. James Wyly, Elmhurst, Illinois
Mr. Rodney Yarbrough, Celina, Texas
Mr. Burton A. Yeager, East Hartford, Connecticut
Mr. Victor I. Zuck, Pittsburgh, Pennsylvania
Mr. Gary Zwicky, East Riverdale, Maryland

CONTENTS

APOLOGIA

ন৯৩

One result of the enlightenment brought about by the *Orgelbe-wegung* or Organ Reform Movement has been the firm re-establishment of two prime requisites for artistic organ building. These are mechanical action and a wooden case.

The worth of an organ depends entirely upon how it sounds when played by a good organist. The Organ Reform Movement sought a return to a rational tonal structure conforming to the *Werkprinzip* or Work Principle. The tonal structure is the first requisite of a good organ; the mechanical action and the wooden case are corollaries.[1]

The organ with an excellent tonal structure but which has one of the available forms of electric key action cannot *sound* as good as it would if it had a well-regulated mechanical key action. With an electrically-controlled key action, the organ virtuoso can produce an attack no different from that produced by a child totally ignorant of music. With mechanical key action, he has control over the attack which immeasurably increases the possibilities of phrasing. This is demonstrable.[2]

The organ with an excellent tonal structure can never *sound* as good when it is in or back of a hole in the wall or even when standing naked on chests spread about the interior of the church as it will when housed in a well-located wooden case. As numerous learned organ builders have emphasized, the case blends and projects the sounds of the pipes. This also is demonstrable.[3]

For at least five centuries, beginning in Gothic times, organ builders incorporated their instruments in free-standing cases. The practice

[1]   This subject is discussed more at length in *The Organ in Church Design* (Venture Press, Albany, Texas, 1957).
[2]   With these differences of attack so easily perceptible, it is surprising that some individuals deny their existence merely because they are insensible to them.
[3]   The two positivs built in my shop have been played in the same room with the pipe-case in place and with it removed. The difference in the tonal quality of each instrument, with and without its case, is pronounced.

of placing unencased organs behind absurd fences of pipes, often all of the same height, and in recesses and chambers outside the church enclosure, did not begin until the latter half of the 19th Century and at first it was only sporadic. By 1925, it had become the universal custom; there was no such thing as contemporary organ cases. Those still in existence from earlier periods were thought of merely as antiques.

To the best of my knowledge, the first modern organ case was that of the Marcussen choir organ in the Grundtvigskirken[4] in Copenhagen which was built in 1940.[5] The wealth of contemporary case design has come about in a period of only twenty-five years and each of the hundred and twelve cases illustrated in this volume was built within the last ten years.

It is no exaggeration to say that organ building in the United States is fully twenty years behind that in Europe. This claim is substantiated by the fact that the organ-building firms which produce all but a minute fraction of the organs built in the United States are still adhering to practices long ago abandoned by the best organ builders in Europe. The backwardness of these American builders, especially in the case of the large commercial organizations, is probably due less to ignorance than to the economic difficulties of a changeover to more progressive and artistic practices.

The one bright spot in this otherwise dismal picture is that small cadre of American builders, young men for the most part, who are producing instruments approaching or equal to the best of Europe.

This activity is stimulated by at least two forces; the growing number of young organists who study in Europe and return with a knowledge of how good organs sound, and the ever-increasing number of good European organs installed in this country.

Its deterrents also are at least two-fold: the opposition of the average American organ-building firm to mechanical action and the

---

[4] Illustrated in *The Organ in Church Design.*
[5] It is my desire always to give credit where credit is due. If I make statements of fact which are actually in error, I trust that a refutation will sooner or later appear in some permanent record.

More and more evidence comes to me that a prime stimulator of organ reform in the United States was the late Melville Smith and I regret that he was not mentioned in my earlier publication while he was yet living; it was simply that I was ignorant of the extent and importance of his influence. There will be serious omissions in this little volume for the same reason. To ferret out the names of designers responsible for many of the meritorious features of cases pictured herein but who are submerged in the anonymity imposed by organizations would require interminable research. Also, it may be assumed that the designs of some of the cases illustrated here were influenced by the work of others quite unknown to me.

In the light of all information I have at hand now, it is my opinion that among organ builders the leader most influential in the resurgence of good organ design was the late Sybrand Zachariassen of Marcussen & Sön, Denmark.

organ case,[6] and the average American church architect's ignorance of and indifference to the problems of good church acoustics and the location and appearance of the organ.[7]

The function of the organ involves only the auditory sense but since the ideal of the function cannot be achieved without a case, the serious organ builder is forced to respond to visual demands.[8] This study is limited to a presentation of contemporary organ case design.[9] It is presumptuous to assume the role of a critic but any uncritical discussion of design is worthless. Many comparisons made and opin-

[6] During the period of questions in a panel discussion at the National Convention of the American Guild of Organists in Detroit in 1960, the president of one of these large firms, when asked what he thought of mechanical-action organs, replied, "They are as wooden as the people who play them." This is typical of the intellectual level of their arguments. It was disclosed in the reappearance this year of the *Organ Institute Quarterly* that the reason for the long gap in its publication was that all the United States manufacturers of electro-pneumatic organs who had been its regular advertising patrons had withdrawn their advertising from that periodical in what appeared to be a concerted action in protest against its advocacy of the modern tracker organ. I do not question the right of advertisers to withdraw their support from any publication they do not like but I am amazed by the shortsightedness of these large commercial companies. Do they actually think they can suppress the dissemination of *all* information on the great strides being made by the progressive organ builders of north Europe? What will they do when they awaken to the fact that, while they were sleeping, their canny old Canadian competitor has greatly outdistanced them by making changeovers for what is inevitable?

[7] These are subjects rather generally ignored in the lectures and seminars of conventions of architects. I have attended two fairly recent Annual Joint Conferences on Church Building and Architecture, sponsored by the Church Architectural Guild of America and the Department of Church Building and Architecture of the National Council of the Churches of Christ in the U.S.A., and have been amazed by the lack of concern of these groups with the real problems of the organ in churches and good church acoustics. It is significant, I think, that G. E. Kidder Smith (Fellow of the American Institute of Architects, member of the General Commission and the Commission on Architecture of the National Council of Churches and contributor of the article on *Religious Architecture* to the Encyclopaedia Britannica) in his new book, *The New Churches of Europe* (Holt, Rinehart Winston; New York, Chicago, San Francisco-1964; sponsored through grants-in-aid by both the Brunner Committee of the New York Chapter of the A.I.A. and the College of Fellows of the A.I.A.), failed to list anything whatsoever on the subject of the organ in his bibliography of some sixty-four books and periodicals on contemporary religious architecture and art. While making this criticism, I am compelled to confess that Joseph Watterson, while editor of the *AIA Journal*, requested me to contribute an article on this subject and, although I promised to do so, I never got around to it; if the new editor will accept my contribution, I hope in the near future to make amends for my failure in duty.

[8] This is not intended to imply that builders of unencased organs need not respond to visual demands; the late Walter Holtkamp was highly successful in composing organs to satisfy the eye as well as to please the ear.

[9] It is self-evident that all the organs discussed cannot have equally good tonal qualities, a subject outside the scope of this work.

ions expressed in this essay will be irritatingly obvious to the good case designer; the well-trained eye needs no guide. Those who are intellectually alive and are interested in but not completely familiar with the elements which compose good case design may be rewarded by following my pointer as we look together at the illustrations.

STYLE

〰

Style evolves from a repetition of characteristics. All works of art are rearrangements of forms, colors, sounds or ideas, either from nature or from previous works, which have been seen or heard by the artist. It is the rearrangements which require the imagination of the artist. It cannot be said that there is style unless these repeated characteristics are recognizable and recognized.[10]

When the same forms supply the inspirations for repetition throughout a field of art or craft, a period style results. When such borrowings are confined within national or regional borders, it can be said that a regional style has been created. Likewise, group styles are formed; in art these usually are given the term *schools*. When one uses his own previous works as inspiration, he soon has a recognizable individual style.[11] While style does not postulate art, every painter, sculptor, writer, composer or architect usually develops a style before he is called an artist. The individual style, like a more encompassing one, can evolve gradually so that its end state is quite distinct from its beginning state. Less frequently, an individual will abruptly change his style. Also, as Dr. Felix Candela has pointed out, repetition breeds symbolism[12] and there is a kind of relationship between symbols and style.

In spite of the rich variety and individuality of today's casework, the contemporary organ case has achieved style. It is interesting, if not remarkable, that a style of great merit should follow, after a

[10] These and the following sentences are a restatement of what has been said by others over and over again; they are reiterated because they give the approach to the comments on the illustrations.
[11] This is a paraphrase of remarks made by Dr. Felix Candela in Dallas last year and which I heard. I thought he used the word *styles* where *structures* appears in the transcript: "Natural evolution is the sound basis for the development of new structures. This is the method followed by recognized structural masters who copy the work of others (or even their own previous works) introducing each time slight improvements and gradual modification of detail. After a time, this routine procedure brings about apparently original results, if we forget the intermediate steps." (Felix Candela: *Structural Form in the Service of Eloquent Architecture* published in the proceedings [p.18] of the Annual Joint Conference on Church Architecture [Dallas, Texas, April 7-9, 1964] sponsored by the Church Architectural Guild of America and the Department of Church Building and Architecture of the National Council of the Churches of Christ in the U.S.A.)
[12] "If we want to establish some formal symbols as characteristic of the assumed new religious spirit, we should be prepared to freeze and repeat a certain structural shape as was done, for instance, in Gothic times . . ." (Ibid. p.18)

dreary hiatus, one so dull as that of the 19th Century. As in the styles of the historic periods, there are within this newest period style national, regional, and individual stylistic trends.

Nearly ninety percent of the organs in the illustrations have cases symmetrical about the vertical axis. In general form they go back to the best of the Gothic and Renaissance examples for inspiration. While the relatively few cases of asymmetrical design show a definite break with historical forms, they have in common with those of the Gothic and Renaissance periods the important qualities of cohesion and integrity and, although theirs is a different branch or substyle from that of the symmetrical cases, they are neither more nor less a part of the contemporary style.

A study of the illustrations will make manifest the debt of today's style to the case designs previous to the middle of the 18th Century, and will make clearer the borrowing, repetition and interplay of ideas and motifs which go to create and develop a new style.

PRESTANTS

ల≁ం

In cases of the historic periods, the façade pipes, called *Prestants*[13] because they stood in front of the other pipes, were of Principal[14] tone. Quite naturally then, by definition, Prestants today are façade pipes of Principal tone. Pipes not in the façade should never be called Prestants, and because centuries of usage have defined Prestants as of Principal tone, façade pipes which are not Principals should not be called Prestants. While the illustrations show that in current usage façade pipes in Prestant position (as differentiated from Spanish Trumpets) are rarely anything but Prestants, there are occasional exceptions.

The Klais organs in St. Dionysius (58)[15] in Gleuel and St. Lamberti (58) in Gladbeck have a complete 16′ Posaune rank in the Pedal façades. The Schmid organ in Trinity Church (72) in Kaufbeuren has reeds set in front of the spaces between longer wooden and metal pipes of the Pedal cases and the same builder uses them in front of the Prestants of the Pedal of St. Bartholomäus (93) in Nürnberg.

Prestants of wide and narrow scale are set alternately in the façades of the division cases in the Rieger organ (83) in the Archiepiscopal Seminary in Cologne. The bottom half of a Subbass 16′ constitutes the front of the Pedal division of the Klais organ (83) in St. Dionysius in Monheim-Baumberg. In Prestant position in the Rückpositiv of the Klais instrument in St. Remigius (52) in Bonn are a five-pipe tower of wooden Gedackt pipes and a flat of Spillpfeife pipes on each side. Their organ in the chapel of St. John's Hospital (59) in Bonn has Untersatz 16′ façade pipes in the Pedal towers and a Salicional 8′ in the Hauptwerk; the latter is of copper in the bottom octave and tin above. Schlicker sets pipes of the Gemshorn 8′ in the fronts of the Pedal cases of the organ in the Lippold studio (89).

Attention is called to these rare exceptions to the use of Prestants as façade pipes merely because they are interesting. The young organ builder should be cautioned not to use pipes other than Prestants in the front position simply for novelty. Tonal design is founded upon the tone color of the Principal and, while I cannot prove it, I am con-

[13] From the Latin *praestans, praestantis:* standing in front of.
[14] The arbitrary style of capitalizing the names of all organ registers and organ divisions has been adopted for this book; many of them are of German origin and, even though most have been taken into the English language, some do not look right without the capital initial. For consistency and to eliminate confusion, this rule has been applied to all, including those of English origin.
[15] Numbers in parentheses refer to the page on which the organ is illustrated.

vinced that there are tonal reasons for placing Principals in the front of the case. The practice has been dictated by the empirical knowledge of the best centuries of organ building.

In the case of almost every exception, a logical reason becomes apparent upon examination of the disposition of the organ. In the organs (58) in Gleuel and Gladbeck,[16] the Posaune resonators are the only pipes of 16' length; to have put the Principal 8' pipes in the façade with the Posaune resonators mitered would have changed radically the relationship of the Pedal cases to the main case. This also is true of the Pedal case of the Klais organ in the Regina Martyrum Church (84) in Berlin-Plötzensee. The Subbass 16' in Monheim-Baumberg (83) is the only rank of 8'-length in the organ. To the school of thought I prefer, the Salicional 8' in the St. John's Hospital organ (59) is superfluous but, if it is to go into the organ at all, it has to have a place. If the Principal 4' were used as a Prestant, where could the Salicional, the only rank in the Hauptwerk of 8'-length, go? It would seem that the designer, in placing it in Prestant position, put it in the only logical place. Since the Lippold organ (89) has no Principal in the Pedal, the Gemshorn 8' makes a good substitute for a Prestant.

It is noteworthy that Spanish Trumpets have become a popular feature of modern encased organs. Only eight years ago, they were limited, I believe, to a few Marcussen cases. The illustrations show their use by eleven of the builders represented here in organs in nine countries; more than a fourth of the organs pictured have them. Twenty-five years ago they would have looked natural only on the Flentrop in Lisbon (76); what might have been considered a Marcussen stylization only a few years ago is now, by adoption, one of the several style characteristics of the contemporary case.[17]

The Flentrop organs in St. Andrew's Church (59) in Malmö and in the Opstandingskerk in Den Helder and the Flentrop-Vermuelen organ in the Church of the Sacrament in Breda[18] all have horizontal reeds in the Pedal only. In Malmö and Breda they are at 4' and 2' and in Den Helder there is a single rank at 4'. The Den Helder and Breda organs were built in 1958.

The next logical development in the use of horizontal reeds in the façade should be a return to the early Iberian practice of placing short-resonator Regals in this position as in the organ in Santa Cruz,

---

[16] The printed disposition of the Gladbeck organ furnished by the builder gives a Principal 16' in the Pedal but obviously it was not in the organ when the photograph was taken.
[17] These reeds, of course, are a part of the tonal design of the organ; it is not my intention to imply that the builder incorporates them for visual effect even though they usually are a striking feature in case design.
[18] Photo and disposition in Kriek and Zandt: *Organum Novum* (Sneek, 1964).

Coimbra,[4] and the north organ in Burgos Cathedral.[4] A start in this direction was made in the Frobenius organ of 1956 in Huddunge, Sweden,[4] which contains a Krummhorn *en chamade;* somewhat similar reeds may be seen flanking the lowest Positiv in the new Flentrop organ (76) in Lisbon Cathedral.[19] It is quite possible that there are other examples of which I am not aware.

The Mounted Cornet, an old compound stop usually associated with French organs, is cropping up more often in contemporary instruments. When it is not hidden by pipe shades, it becomes a secondary part of the façade pipework. Mounted Cornets may be seen in the Rückpositivs of the Klais organs in Himmerod-Eifel (60) and Karlsruhe-Mühlburg (80) and in the Hauptwerk at Wesseling-Süd (80).[20]

Doubled treble Prestants are appearing more and more in contemporary organs. Joining the toes (with the wind tubed directly into the pipe backs), as in the façade of the Zorgvlietkerk organ (49) in Scheveningen, has ample precedents in organs dating back to Gothic times but it was a tour de force some five centuries ago in Rhenen[4] and it is, I believe, still one today.[21] I do not mean to be faultfinding

---

[19] For many months I have had sets of German Regals in my shop for use in the façades of positivs which I have designed but not built.

[20] The first is of four ranks and the other two of three ranks which would necessitate drawing an independent 8' with the first and an independent 8' and 4' with the other two to complete the full Cornet.

[21] I reserve the right to change my opinions. An unfortunate thing about putting opinions into print is that they tend to become solidified, like concrete, not in the writer's own mind but in the reader's idea of what the writer thinks, and this is a perfectly natural thing, for the reader who reads a statement five years after it was written, but who has no knowledge of subsequent statements of the writer, looks upon it as indelible.

All new experience and new information either confirm or color or change one's opinions. I consider myself a continuing student of organ matters and it happens that my studies, research and experimentation during the eight years since publication of *The Organ in Church Design* have confirmed nearly all the opinions expressed there but not *all*.

For example, at the Organ Symposium of the Central Lutheran Church of Minneapolis, in connection with their annual Organ and Choral Festival held in May, 1965, in which Frederic Hilary graciously had invited me to participate, Lawrence Phelps, while on the subject of the order of ranks in his most interesting and scholarly paper on the *Werkprinzip*, interrupted to say that he was not in agreement with my suggestion that the Principals be placed at the back of the chest. He was referring to the following from *The Organ in Church Design:*

"*It remains for some organ builder and architect to carry these ideas to their logical conclusion which is an organ with all divisions encased according to the* Werkprinzip *but with the front pipes eliminated by moving them to the back of the chest and thus disclosing the terraced ranks of smaller pipes.*

"*By making this suggestion to organ builders and church designers, I do not advocate the suppression of front pipes in all organs. This merely would open*

with respect to a case as stunning as this one—it is just that I have the kind of eye that prefers a toeboard between the doubles as in the examples in Nieuwendijk (48) and Groningen (56).

In the purest application of the work principle to organ design, the tonal structure of each division is based upon a Principal of different pitch from the foundation Principal of any other division, and in its purest application to case design, the Principal upon which each division is based is expressed in the façade of that particular division. On examination, however, it will be seen that the Brustwerk rarely has a Prestant in the façade. This division often has Swell shades, especially in Germany and the United States; when there is no Swell, one can see that the smaller pipes are more often at the front than not. I believe the sole purpose of this sequence is to provide access for the tuner.

The scale relationships of the divisions of an organ designed on this principle may be seen in the façade of the van Vulpen organ in Our Lady of Mount Carmel (54) in Amstelveen. Although the base Principal of the Brustwerk is called (according to Dutch custom) Prestant 2', it is not in the Brust façade, as can be seen in the illustration, but farther back. The Rückpositiv has a Prestant 4', the Hauptwerk a Prestant 8' and the Pedal a Prestant 16'. Each division has a well developed Principal chorus.

This façade expresses the tonal framework of the organ. Case design at its best should tell the viewer something of the character

up a new field in the architectural treatment of the organ and one wholly compatible with current trends in architectural design. If handled imaginatively, it could be an interesting development in the visual design of organs."

These two paragraphs followed a specific reference to the two cases in the Schlicker organ of 1954[4] in Trinity Episcopal Church, Buffalo, New York.

I was quick to reply to Mr. Phelps that I was in complete agreement with him. In each of the two positivs which I have built, one in 1960 which I designed and one in 1963 in which George L. Bozeman, Jr., collaborated, the order of ranks back of the Prestant was from largest to smallest. Since 1957, I have learned that the old builders had an excellent reason for this order just as they had an excellent reason for their cases; the upperwork ranks blend better when they are behind.

Also, when I designed the case for the organ in the Matthews Memorial Presbyterian Church in Albany, Texas, which was finished in 1955 (the design was about 1953), I simply did not know that each division should be in a separate compartment; Mr. Flentrop, who collaborated with Mr. Hofmann in building the organ, was disappointed when he learned there were no partitions between the Hauptwerk and the Pedal towers.

So, gentle reader, please allow me the privilege of learning and changing my mind. The fact that nearly all the opinions I put into print in 1957 have stood up is of no particular credit to me for I was merely trying to pass on to the architectural profession what I had learned from some of the best organ builders of the world and from some enlightened organists and writers.

of the instrument behind it just as a man's face gives at least a hint of the character behind it. The most eloquent constituent at the case designer's disposal is that of the Prestants.[22]

<hr>

[22] The elements of case design have been defined, described and discussed at some length in *The Organ in Church Design* and since it can be found in libraries throughout the English-speaking world, I shall try to repeat as little as possible. For the most part, the terminology used is explained by the illustrations which are the more important part of this volume.

DESIGN COMPONENTS OF THE PRESTANT

❧

The most favored metal for Prestants has for centuries been tin and the illustrations show that it has maintained its position in contemporary organs. Because of the high cost and softness of tin, large pipes are often made of copper or zinc. Numerous examples of copper pipes may be found in the illustrations. Before delivery to and as specified by the pipemaker, copper, more often than not, is treated with brine or heat to produce a surface mottling of rich colors. An example easily seen in the photograph is that of the Pedal pipes in the Leeflang organ (51) in the Immanuelkerk in Delft. The zinc Prestants of today's organs are not of the dark color to which we have been accustomed but are of electrolytic zinc which has a bright silvery matte sheen. The Prestants in the Pedal towers of the von Beckerath organ (73) in St. Andreas, Hildesheim, appear to be of this material.

More rarely, spotted metal (an alloy of tin and lead containing a higher percentage of lead than the alloy of very high tin content referred to simply as tin) is used for Prestants; spotted metal Prestants are more likely to be encountered in England and the United States than on the European continent. The Prestants of the Hill, Norman & Beard nave organ (77) in Bradford Cathedral are spotted metal. The spotted surface is sometimes planed off the metal before the pipes are formed; when it is left in its natural state as in the Bradford example, the texture of the pipes' surface is quite different from that of a polished tin pipe.

The form of the pipe mouth is another component of the Prestant with which the designer can play to give added interest to his design. Contemporary builders employ all the forms common to historic organs. In general the upper lip is either pointed or round or simply pressed into the pipe. The pointed and round lips may be made separately and of a different metal from that of the pipe and soldered on, or they may be an integral part of the pipe in which case they are formed by scoring the underside of the metal. Copper pipes often have tin mouths soldered on. Such mouths with round upper lips may be seen on the Pedal Prestants in St. Remigius, Bonn (52); pointed upper lips usually are of moderate height as in the Immanuelkerk Prestants in Delft (51), but sometimes they are elongated as in the Prestants of St. Andrew's Church in Malmö (59). The latter form is sometimes called "the English bay leaf mouth." The soldered-on mouths often have cusped lips; the 16'-C pipe in the organ in St. Suitbertus (58) in Remscheid stands on an angle which clearly shows the cusps of the upper and lower lips. Lips which are pressed down may be seen throughout the façade of the Hammarberg organ (67) in Sävedalen.

More than one type of pipe mouth is used in some instances not only in the same organ but in a single grouping of pipes. An example is the Kuhn organ (46) in Schüttorf in which only the center pipes of each tower have round upper lips.

Centuries of case design established this rule for Prestants: *either the length of the feet should be a constant or the length of the foot should increase as the speaking length of the pipe decreases.* The most notable of the rare exceptions to this rule in old organs is that of the great case in the Cathedral of Amiens.[4] One will find numerous violations among the cases illustrated but it cannot be broken with impunity for in each instance it has been detrimental in some degree to the architectural scale of the case.

Top flight case designers will disregard this rule with the willingness of sacrificing in architectural scale what they believe they gain in composition through the resulting lines of pipe mouths. Violations of rules should be left to the experts.

A study of the illustrations will show the wide latitude of design afforded by the actual components of Prestant construction: the metal, the lips and the feet. In only a small percentage of contemporary organs has the designer gone beyond these and then he has entered the area of decoration, a legitimate adjunct to but not an essential of good design.

DECORATION OF THE PRESTANT

ᕧᕧᕧ

A very old form of pipe decoration is that of embossing the metal as was done in the organs[4] in Jutphaas, Netherlands, Old Radnor, Wales, and numerous other old organs. The center Salicional in the St. John's Hospital organ (59) in Bonn and several pipes in both the great and Rückpositiv cases of the organ in the Zorgvlietkerk (49) in Scheveningen are embossed. The resulting waviness of the upper lips, similar to that of the center pipe of the mid-16th Century organ in Monnikendam[4] and a few other old organs, is clearly defined in the Zorgvlietkerk examples. Though difficult to make out in the illustration, all the pipes in the center compartments of both Hauptwerk and Rückpositiv of the organ in Trinity Church (72) in Kaufbeuren are embossed.

Embossed pipes give a rich embellishment to a case façade but the designer should bear in mind that they are expensive.

Painted designs on Prestants, a decorative device rare in older organs but extremely popular in English and American organs of the Victorian period, was introduced into contemporary design by Marcussen & Sön. In the Victorian organs, the large front pipes were customarily made of zinc, had false lengths and were painted in their entirety; the stencilled designs were usually but not invariably crude in both color and form. Painted designs on Prestants of Marcussen organs have been confined almost invariably to copper pipes. It seems akin to sacrilege to apply decorative designs in color to tin pipes; the only example known to me is that of the three-manual Marcussen organ of 1960 in Sct. Pauls Kirke, Aarhus, Denmark, which has gold decorations on the tin Prestants. The case design is by Aksel Skov, architect. Among the organs illustrated, the only exception to copper as a background for painting is that of the Pedal Prestants of the von Beckerath organ in Hildesheim (73).

The four Marcussen organs included here which have painted Prestants are those in the Nicolaikerk, Utrecht, Netherlands (56), the Klosterkirken, Lund, Sweden (70), the Vor Frue Kirke, Vordingborg, Denmark (71) and Sct. Mikkels Kirke, Slagelse, Denmark (71). Mr. P. G. Andersen, who collaborated in the designing of these cases also had a hand in the design of the Metzler organ in the Grossmünster in Zürich, Switzerland (57), which, other than the von Beckerath example, is the only contemporary case with painted Prestants not built by Marcussen which has come to my attention.

Probably the first modern case having Prestants with this form of decoration is that of the Marcussen organ[4] of 1944 in the church in Jaegersborg, a suburb of Copenhagen. The highly stylized faces on the mouths of the Utrecht Nicolaikerk Prestants (56) are reminiscent of the grotesque faces on the Prestants of old organs in Lübeck, Spain and Mexico.[4]

Gold leaf or other gilding is sometimes applied to Prestants as well as to the resonators of Spanish Trumpets, as in the organs of the Reformed Church, Nieuwendijk (48), and the Zorgvlietkerk, Scheveningen (49). The Prestants of the Pniëlkerk, Apeldoorn (50), have gold leaf on the lips.

PIPE SHADES

⟡

The oldest known organ case in existence, that in Ste. Catherine's[4] in Sion, Switzerland, contained pipe shades; in the Gothic and each succeeding architectural period, pipe shades have taken multiple forms. As great a variety can be found in today's cases as in those of all previous periods collectively.

Pipe shades are not a necessary part of an organ case. D. A. Flentrop and Johannes Klais, two of the larger firms, rarely use them. When they are omitted, the dark voids, forming a backdrop for the Prestants, become an element of the design. The purpose of shades, obviously, is to fill the space above the tops of the pipes. Unless they improve the appearance of the organ, they should be left out of the design for they add to the cost of the case. Sometimes too much light will fall on pipes back of the Prestants, making them show distractingly above the Prestants, or windtrunks or other unsightly components may be seen; by screening these from view, pipe shades tie the façade together and make the composition complete. Even when the ratio of voids to solids is large, as in the Marcussen organ in the Mariehöj Kirke (53) in Silkeborg, they present a surface over which the eye can play. Sometimes they are there merely for the sake of decoration or they may be there because the designer, like the ancient Egyptians, suffered from *horror vacui*.

Pipe shades may be placed in a plane in front of the pipes, overlapping the tops so that they either hide or partially screen the tops, or in a plane back of the pipes so that the pipe tops are silhouetted against the shades, or they may be set in the plane of the pipes clear of the tops. This third position precludes cone tuning. They are usually either in front or back of the pipes. When in the latter position, they are nearly always airy grilles of flat surfaced fretwork; more often than not, the fretwork is of simple geometric design. This use of pipe shades, like their total absence, emphasizes the pipe tops but, unlike the voids, gives the designer the tools of both surface and color.

Ernst Leeflang has used two different and most effective types of pipe shades in the plane back of the pipes. Those in the Pniëlkerk in Apeldoorn (50) are made up of narrow strips of wood in a random web-like system of lines with scroll-saw birds applied to them. They are decorated with red, blue and gold; the large dark voids surrounding them enrich the colors. Several of the old cases, that in Roskilde[4] for example, were embellished with their dates painted on in decorative letters and numerals. Here wooden ones have been applied between the smallest Prestants.[23]

Those in the Immanuelkerk in Delft (51) have been cut from plywood with the ratio of solids to voids much larger than at Apeldoorn and there is no applied color. It will be remembered that many old organs had space fillers between the Prestant feet; those between the Pedal Prestant toes are the only ones I remember ever having seen in a contemporary case. Here, as in Apeldoorn, cutout birds have been applied.

Several organs, not illustrated, by other Dutch builders have shades cut out by scroll saw. Those in Nieuwendijk (48) and Scheveningen (49), in front of the plane of pipes, are akin to the shades in the Immanuelkerk organ in Delft but they have a lightly carved relief.

The shades carved by J. Seldenthuis of Utrecht for the Hammarberg organs[24] illustrated on pages 67, 68 and 69 are different from those in Arnhem (42); with the exception of the Sävedalen (67) shades which have a regular pattern, they are unique in character and seem almost a hallmark of Hammarberg casework. (The scale of those in Vollsjö (67) is perhaps too heavy and the pipelike forms in the Brust are, I feel, an inadvisable motif for an organ façade.) All of them are both rich and contemporary in quality.

The allover pattern of the shades in the van Vulpen case in Our Lady of Mount Carmel, Amstelveen (54), somewhat reminiscent of that in the Alice Millar Chapel, Evanston (75), are scaled to each of the four divisions. Those of the Marcussen organ in Christian X's Mindekirke, Sönderborg (55), are interestingly scaled to each Prestant throughout the façades of both Rückpositiv and main cases. Not only are they original in their frank asymmetry but they also bear a studied relation to the surrounding brick work. The case design is by the son of the architect of the church building.

After the new choir organ in the Minster of Ulm (45) was installed, the authorities caused the pipe shades to be removed. When they were out, they realized they were needed and requested Mr. von Glatter-Götz to replace them. My photos were made before those of the main case had been put back; the view from the nave shows how necessary they are to fill the profile gaps between Prestants and case top in the towers. The tower of the Rückpositiv looks complete; those of the main case do not.

---

[23] Apparently, the finishing touches were not put on this organ until 1962, the year of completion given me.

[24] As in the destroyed organ[4] in the Marienkirche in Dortmund, that in the Simrishamn Kyrka (69) has the key desk on the side of the case. In Dortmund, it was on the left; here it is on the right.

No little part of the effect of the façade of the Metzler organ[25] in the Grossmünster (57) in Zürich is derived from the angels applied to the shades; as additional decoration there are shields bearing the arms of the parish and city of Zürich. Shields are also used most effectively across the top of the Great case of the organ in the Alice Millar Chapel (75); there they carry the symbols of the Persons of the Trinity and the twelve apostles.

The variety of treatments of pipe shades represented in the illustrations should afford limitless stimulation to the case designer's imagination.

[25] Most of the factual data in this book concerning the Grossmünster in Zürich was obtained from W. L. Sumner's article, *The Organ in the Grossmünster, Zürich* in *The Organ* for July, 1962 (Musical Opinion, London). I did not make notes while I was in the Grossmünster as I expected to obtain the data from the builder later; in this I failed. Mr. Sumner names the several individuals who had a part in the design and decoration of the case.

30

SHUTTERS

The ancient practice of placing shutters on cases has by no means become extinct. More than twenty percent of the organs illustrated have them on one case or another; in many they are limited to the Brustwerk. The organ in the Zorgvlietkerk (49) in Scheveningen has shutters, each with two leaves, which will completely enclose both the Hauptwerk and Rückpositiv cases. Those of the organ in Kappel (34) are unusually interesting in that each has four leaves and they are so hinged that when completely folded, the top of each successive leaf can be seen above the one in front. The shutters are no little part of the striking aplomb of this design.

The great single-leaf shutters in the Cloister of St. Trudpert (60), about twenty-two feet high, seem to be reaching for the heavens; they are reminiscent of the monumental shutters of old organs like that in the Cathedral of Tarragona.[4]

The large organ in Silkeborg (53) has shutters for every division but the Hauptwerk. The shutters of the Brustwerk in the Alice Millar Chapel (75), hardly visible in the illustration, are actually Swell shades operated from the console.

Many small organs which have no Swell have shutters only for the Positiv division as in the organs in Mesquite (86) and Arnhem (42) which have shutters for the Brust, and those (96) in Montevallo and Winston-Salem where the Rückpositiv is shuttered. In such situations, the organist sometimes presets the shutters for a particular effect in the same way some organists use Swell shades as an aid to registration rather than so-called expression.

In the historic periods, shutters were areas to be decorated and some exhibited the handiwork of painters of some note. Today they are rarely ornamented.

THE CYMBELSTERN

❧

The Cymbelstern or bell-star, an old and merry device, has not been discarded completely. There are two in the Zorgvlietkerk organ (49); although scarcely discernible in the photograph, the stars are in front of the pipe shades of the outer flats. There are also two in the organ in Trinity Church (72) in Kaufbeuren; one is in the Hauptwerk and the other in the Rückpositiv with its five-pointed star showing just above the case. That in Grand Forks (94) is a prominent feature of the façade. One may be seen in front of the center Prestant of the Hauptwerk in the Nicolaikerk (56) in Utrecht.

THE ILLUSTRATIONS

Where case designs are by the builders of the organs, names in parentheses indicate the individual in the firm most responsible for the design. The overall dimensions of cases are taken to the nearest inch.

Montreal, Quebec, Canada; Sanctuaire Marie-Reine-des-Coeurs (contemporary); Casavant Frères organ, 1965, 2 manuals, 56 notes, 29 registers, 39 ranks, mechanical key and stop action; case design by the builder (Karl Wilhelm); height 23′, width 20′, depth 4′; Rückpositiv case: height 7′-6″, width 8′-0″, depth 3′-6″; wood: oak; location: the center of the rear gallery

Kappel, Albis, Switzerland; former Klosterkirche Zisterzienser (15th Cent.); Th. Kuhn organ, 1963, 2 manuals, 56 notes, 16 registers, 23 ranks, mechanical key and stop action; case design: Paul Hintermann, architect; H 16'-5", W 9'-2", D 3'-3"; wood: oak; location: about midway in the nave arcade

Beaumont, Texas; Bethlehem Lutheran Church (1963), architect: D. Rex Goode; Hofmann organ, 1964, 2 manuals, 56 notes, 15 registers, 21 ranks, mechanical key action, electric stop action; case design: builder; H 18', W 13', D 11' with console; wood: mahogany, walnut, fir; location: in the rear gallery

Joliette, Quebec, Canada: Seminaire de Joliette Chapel; Casavant Frères organ, 1962, 2 manuals, 56 notes, 24 registers, 32 ranks, mechanical key and stop action; case design by Casavant (Karl Wilhelm); H 20'-9", W 18'-6", D 6'-9"; wood: oak; location: on the nave floor at the rear of the chapel

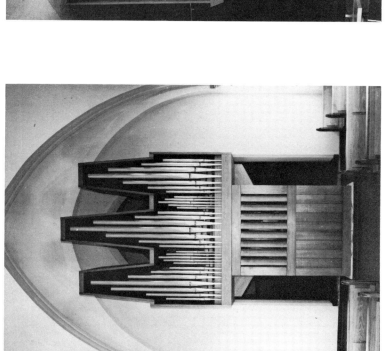

Düsseldorf-Bilk, Germany; St. Martinn's Krankenhaus (c.1900); Klais organ, 1965, 2 manuals, 56 notes, 12 registers, 16-17 ranks, mechanical key action, electric stop action; case design by the builder; H 21'-9", W 11'-2", D 3'-7"; wood: oak; location: between the nave and the nuns' choir

35

Spring Valley, New York; St. Paul's Episcopal Church (c. 1895) Gress-Miles organ, 1960, 2 manuals, 58 notes, 10 registers, 14 ranks, electric key and stop action; case design: builder; height 14', width 8', depth 6'; wood: walnut; location: at the rear wall of the nave

Portland, Oregon; St. Stephen's Cathedral (Episcopal) (c. 1900) Gress-Miles organ, 1965, 2 manuals, 58 notes, 11 registers, 16 ranks, electric key and stop action; case design by builder; height 18', width 10', depth 6'; wood: walnut; location: at the right front of the nave

Woodlawn, New York; St. Stephen's Episcopal Church (c. 1900); Gress-Miles organ, 1960, 2 manuals, 58 notes, 13 registers, 17 ranks, electric key and stop action; case design: by the builder; height 13', width 8', depth 4'-6'; wood: walnut; location: at the Gospel side of the chancel

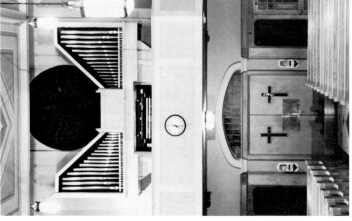

Glasgow, Scotland; Kings Park R. C. Church (1960), Thomas Cordiner, architect; Hill, Norman & Beard organ, 1961, 2 manuals, 61 notes, 14 registers, 9 ranks; electric action; case design: builder and architect; height 20', width 8'-6", depth 5'-6"; wood: mahogany; location: the rear gallery

Bad Kohlgrub, Germany; Evangelische Kirche (1936); Gerhard Schmid organ, 1963, 2 manuals, 56 notes, 10 registers, 13 ranks, mechanical key and stop action; case design by builder; height 10'-6", width 6'-3", depth 3'-3" (RP 1'-4"); wood: larch; location: in the choir

Tuckahoe, New York; Church of the Assumption (c.1890), organ by Delaware Organ Co., 1963, 2 manuals, 61 notes, 19 registers, 25 ranks, electro-pneumatic action; case design: builder; center case H 11'-6", W 14', D 2'-6"; wood: natural red oak; location: in the rear gallery

37

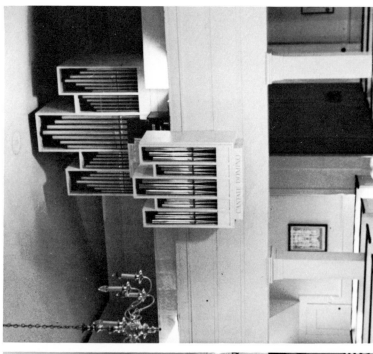

Stamford, Connecticut; St. Francis' Episcopal Church (1834); organ by Van Zoeren, Henderson & Steinkampf, 1963, 2 manuals, 58 notes, 32 registers (unified), direct electric key and stop action; case design by Richard Henderson, architect; main case: H 8'-7", W 6'-5", D 3'-6"; Rückpositiv: H 3'-6", W 3'-6", D 1'-6"; wood: white pine; location: in the rear gallery

Batesville, Arkansas; Christian Science Church (1957), building designed by Allen L. Crouch, III, and Peter McManus; D. A. Flentrop organ, 1960, 2 manuals, 56 notes, 20 registers, 26-27 ranks, mechanical key action, mechanical stop action; case design by the builder, main case: height 15'-7", width 13'-4", depth 2'-8"; wood: mahogany; location: in the rear gallery

Yonkers, New York; Church of Our Lady of Mount Carmel (older); organ built by the Delaware Organ Company, 1964, 61 notes, 23 registers, 24 ranks, electro-pneumatic action; case design by the Delaware Organ Company; height 21'-9", width 14'-6", depth 5'-6"; width at the floor level: 8'-3"; wood: natural oak; interior painted deep blue; location: center of the rear gallery

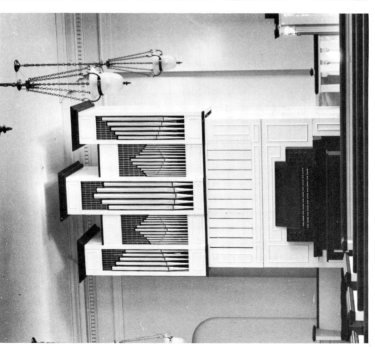

Tyler, Texas; Chapel, First Presbyterian Church (1951). Mark Lemmon, architect; organ by Robert L. Sipe, Inc., 1965, 2 manuals, 61 notes, 12 registers, 14 ranks, mechanical key and stop action; case design by the builder (George L. Bozeman, Jr.), height 14'-11", width 7'-7" depth 5'-1"; wood: painted birch with Honduras mahogany trim; location: in the front center

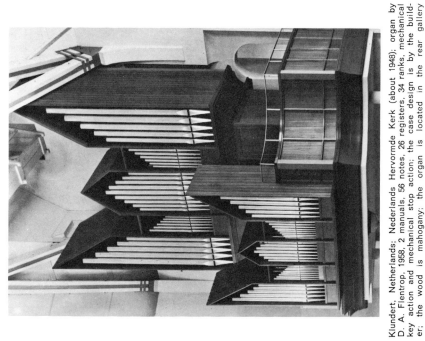

Klundert, Netherlands; Nederlands Hervormde Kerk (about 1948); organ by D. A. Flentrop, 1958, 2 manuals, 56 notes, 26 registers, 34 ranks, mechanical key action and mechanical stop action; the case design is by the builder; the wood is mahogany; the organ is located in the rear gallery

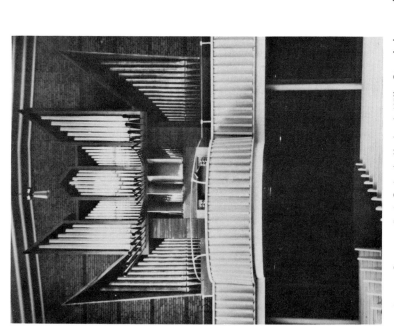

Hamburg-Altona, Germany; Paul Gerhardt Kirche (c.1950), Otto Andersen, architect; Flentrop organ, 1960, 2 manuals, 56 notes, 24 registers, 34 ranks, mechanical key and stop action; case design by builder and architect; H 24'-4'', W 24'-4'', D 3'-3''; wood: mahogany; location: in the rear gallery

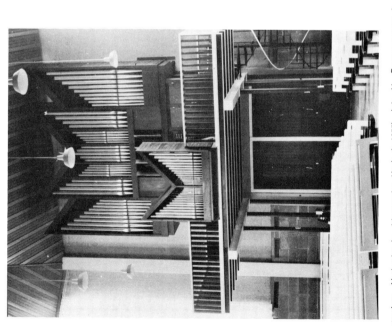

Amsterdam, Netherlands: Maranatha Kerk (c.1955), Joh. H. Groenewegen & H. Mieras, architects; Flentrop organ, 1959, 3 manuals, 56 notes, 31 registers, 42-43 ranks, mechanical key & stop action; case: builder with architects; H 21'-6", W 17'-7", D 3'-3"; location: in the west gallery

Seattle, Washington; Episcopal Cathedral; D. A. Flentrop organ, 1965, 4 manuals, 56 notes, 55 registers, 72 ranks, mechanical key action, electric stop action; case design by builder (I. A. Steketee); height 46'-7", width 33'-2", depth 4'-2"; wood: mahogany; location: in the gallery

41

Arnhem, Netherlands; St. Eusebiuskerk (Gothic); van Vulpen organ, 1961, 2 manuals, 54 notes, 15 registers, 18-20 ranks, mechanical key and stop action; case design by the builder; dimensions comparable to those on the facing page; wood: oak; location: in the choir arcade

Bodenwerder, Germany; St. Maria Königin (contemporary); Johannes Klais organ, 1963, 2 manuals, 56 notes, 12 registers, 16 ranks, mechanical key and stop action; case design by the builder; height 18'-1", width 10'-6", depth 3'-11"; wood: oak; location: in the rear balcony

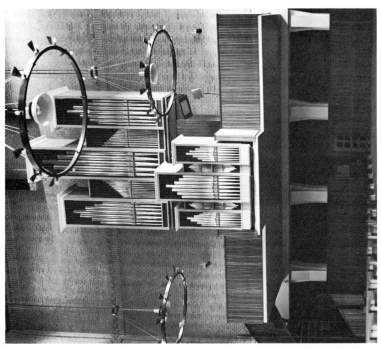

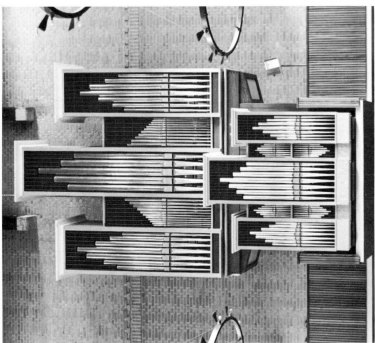

The Hague, Netherlands; Nederlands Hervormde Pauluskerk (1954), Prof. Ir. J. F. Berghoef, architect; Gebr. van Vulpen organ, 1962, 2 manuals, 54 notes, 19 registers, 25-28 ranks, mechanical key and stop action; case design by the builder; wood: oak; the organ is located in the rear gallery

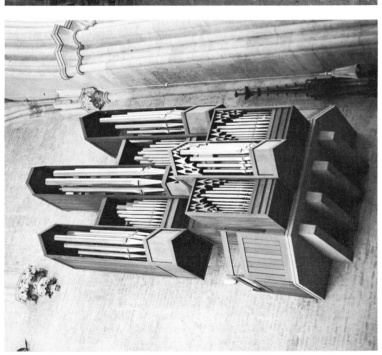

Ulm, Germany; the Cathedral of Ulm (Gothic, 14th-16th Cent.); the organ was built by Rieger and completed about 1964; the case design is by the builder (Ingenieur Josef von Glatter-Götz); the resources are comparable to those of the organ on the facing page; location: south wall of the choir

45

Schüttorf, Grafschaft Bentheim, Germany; Reformierte Kirche Schüttorf (14th Cent.); organ by Th. Kuhn AG, 1963, 2 manuals, 56 notes, 26 registers, 38-40 ranks, mechanical key and stop action; case design by the builder; H 18'-4", W 9'-10", D 3'-7"; wood: oak; location: in the gallery

Marknesse, Netherlands; Gereformeerd Kerk (c.1960), Theo G. Verlaan, architect; D. A. Flentrop organ, 1961, 2 manuals, 56 notes, 10 registers, 13 ranks, mechanical key action, mechanical stop action; height 12'-11", width 5'-10", depth 2'-4"; wood: mahogany; location: in the gallery

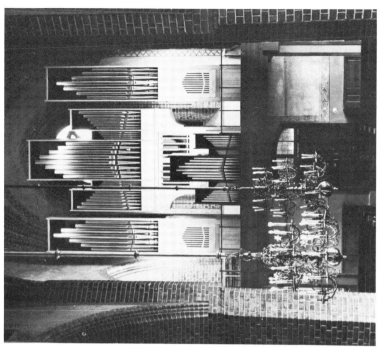

Falun, Sweden; Stora Kopparsbergs Kirke (Gothic building), organ built by Th. Frobenius & Co., completed in 1963, 3 manuals, 56 notes, 31 registers, about 40 ranks, mechanical key action and mechanical stop action; case design is by Th. Frobenius & Co.; wood: oak; location: in the rear gallery

Lingen, Ems, Germany; St. Maria Königin (contemporary). Dipl. Ing. Burlage and Niebuer, architects; Johannes Klais organ, 1963, 3 manuals, 21 registers, 29-31 ranks, mechanical key and stop action; case design by the builder; H 23′, D 3′-3′; wood: oak; location: in the rear gallery

47

Nieuwendijk, Netherlands; Gerefomeerd Kerk (an older building); organ built by Gebr. van Vulpen completed in 1960, 2 manuals, 54 notes, 23 registers, 37-39 ranks, mechanical key action and mechanical stop action; case design by the builder; the overall dimensions are comparable to those of the case on the facing page; wood: solid Oregon pine; location: rear gallery

Scheveningen, Netherlands; Nederlands Hervormde Zorgvlietkerk (contemporary): Ahrend & Brunzema organ, 1959, 3 manuals, 54 notes, 26 registers, 31-34 ranks, mechanical key and stop action; case design by builder; height 18'-11", width 11'-1", depth 3'-2"; Rückpositiv height 5'-9", width 5'-9", depth 2'-1"; wood: oak; location: in the rear gallery off center

49

Apeldoorn, Netherlands; Nederlands Hervormde Pniëlkerk (contemporary), architect: Ir. G.
Pothoven; Ernst Leeflang organ, 1962, 2 manuals, 54 notes, 12 registers, 14 ranks, mechanical key and stop action; case design by the builder (Jan Keijzer); overall dimensions:
height 15'-3", width 11'-4", depth 2'-7"; wood: Slavic oak; location: in the gallery

50

Delft, Netherlands; Gereformeerd Immanuëlkerk (contemporary), architect: Prof. F. A. Eschauzier; Leeflang organ, 1963, 3 manuals, 56 notes, 34 registers, 59 ranks, all mechanical action; case design: builder (Jan Keijzer); H 23'-2", W 19'-3", D 4'-3", Hauptwerk D 3'-2"; Rückpositiv: H 6'-1", W 6'-1", D 3'-1"; wood: Sipo-mahogany; location: in the rear gallery

Bonn, Germany; St. Remigius (old); organ built by Johannes Klais in 1963, 3 manuals, 56 notes, 32 registers, 46-48 ranks, mechanical key action, electric stop action, case design by the builder; overall dimensions of main case height 27'-11", width 23'-0", depth 4'-3"; wood: solid oak lightly stained; the organ is located in the rear gallery

Silkeborg, Denmark; Mariehöj Kirke (contemporary), architect: Viggo Hardie-Fischer; Marcussen organ, 1965, 3 manuals, 56 notes, 32 registers, 45 ranks; mechanical key and stop action; case design by the architect; height 29'-0", width 14'-7", depth 2'-9", Pedal depth 4'-2"; Rückpositiv: width 6'-4", depth 2'-6"; wood: oak; location: in the rear gallery

Amstelveen, Netherlands; Roman Catholic Carmelkerk (1964), architects: Sips and Molenaar; Gebr. van Vulpen organ, 1965, 3 manuals, 54 notes, 31 registers, 45-46 ranks; mechanical key action and mechanical stop action; the case design is by the builder; overall height about 24', overall width about 18'; wood: solid oak unpainted; location: in the rear gallery

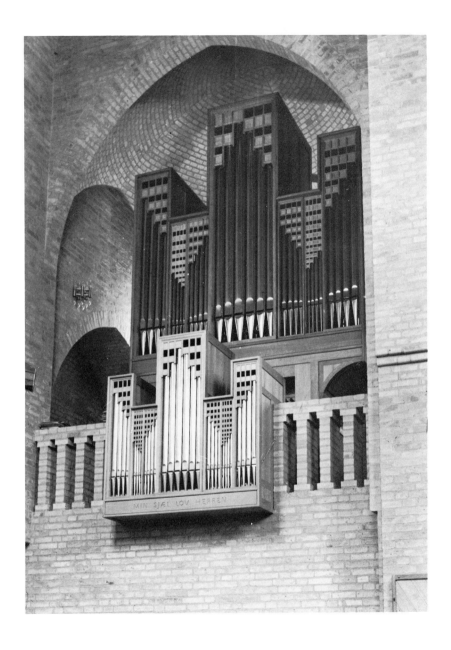

Sönderborg, Denmark; Christian X's Mindekirke (contemporary), architect: Kaare Klint; Marcussen organ, 1959, 2 manuals, 56 notes, 22 registers, 29 ranks, mechanical key and stop action; case design by Esben Klint, architect; height 16'-11", width 9'-7", depth 6'-1"; Rückpositiv: width 5'-5", depth 2'-6"; wood: oak; location: in a side gallery at the rear

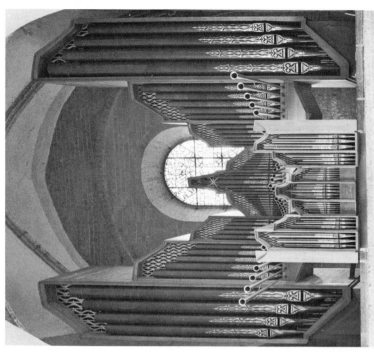

Utrecht, Netherlands: St. Nicolai Kerk (old): Marcussen & Son organ, 1956; 3 manuals, 54 notes, 33 registers, 50-54 ranks, mechanical key and stop action; case design by the builder (P. G. Andersen); H 22′, W 19′-3″, D 4′-11″; Pedal: D 2′-11″; wood: oak; location: in the rear gallery

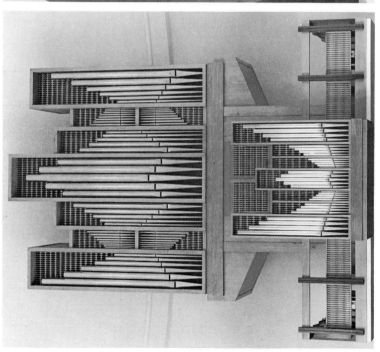

Groningen, Netherlands: Doopsgezinde Kerk: organ by Marcussen & Son, 1961, 3 manuals, 56 notes, 24 registers, 29-31 ranks, mechanical key and stop action; case design by the builder; H 21′-11″, W 12′-6″, D 3′-7″; Rückpositiv case: W 5′-6″, D 2′-6″; wood: oak; location: in a small gallery

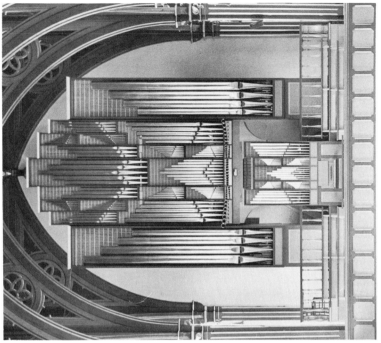

Fredrikstad, Norway; Vestsidens Kirke (c.1870); Marcussen & Sön organ, 1964, 4 manuals, 56 notes, 54 registers, 76-78 ranks, mechanical key action, electric stop action; case design: builder (Br. Christensen); H 29'-10", W 18'-6", D 5'-1", RP D 3'-3"; wood: painted pine; location: the rear gallery

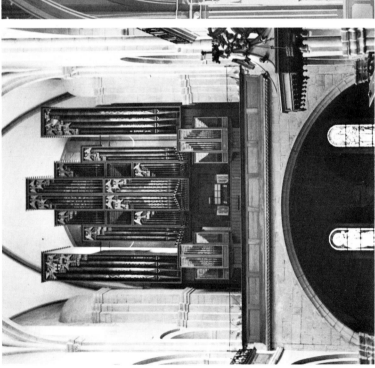

Zürich, Switzerland; Grossmünster (Romanesque, Gothic and later); Metzler organ, 1960, 4 manuals, 56 notes, 67 registers, 92-93 ranks, mechanical key action, electric stop action, case design by Paul Hintermann, architect, in collaboration with others; location: in the rear gallery

Remscheid, Germany; St. Suitbertus (neo-Gothic); Klais organ, 1962, 3 manuals, 56 notes, 33 registers, 46-47 ranks, mechanical key action, electric stop action; case design: Klais; height 23', width 23', depth 4'-3"; wood: oak; location: in the rear gallery

Dernbach, Westerwald, Germany; Mutterhaus der A. D. J. Christi (old); Klais organ, 1963, 2 manuals, 56 notes, 16 registers, 20 ranks, mechanical key action, electric stop action; case: Klais; H 16'-5", W 10'-6", D 3'-11"; wood: oak; location: rear gallery

Gleuel über Köln, Germany; St. Dionysius (neo-Gothic); Klais organ, 1962, 2 manuals, 56 notes, 23 registers, 31 ranks, mechanical key action, electric stop action; case design: Klais; H 22'-4", W 21'-4", D 3'-11"; wood: natural oak; location: rear gallery

Gladbeck, Germany; St. Lamberti (neo-Gothic); Klais organ, 1960, 3 manuals, 56 notes, 36 registers, 50 ranks, mechanical key action, electric stop action; case design: Klais; H 23', W 32'-10", D 4'-3"; white with red and gold; location: in the rear gallery

58

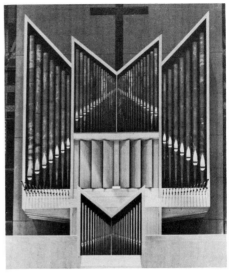

Leidschendam, Netherlands; "Hulp en Heil" Chapel, Alb. van Essen, architect; Flentrop organ, 1962, 2 manuals, 54 notes, 20 registers, 24 ranks; all mechanical action; case: architect & builder; H 20', W 17'-5", D 3'-3"; wood: mahogany; location: rear gallery

Malmö, Sweden; Slottstadens St. Andreas Kyrka, Roos & Thornberg, architects; Flentrop organ, 1961, 3 manuals, 56 notes, 41 registers, 57-58 ranks, all mechanical action; case design: architects & builder; H 30', W 21'-8"; D 3'-11"; location: the rear gallery

Heiligenhaus, Germany; St. Ludgerus (c.1958), A. Leitl, architect; Klais organ, 1965, 2 manuals, 56 notes, 20 registers, 28-31 ranks, mechanical key and electric stop action; case: Klais; H 20', W 12', D 6'; wood: natural pine; location: the rear gallery

Bonn, Germany; St. Johanneshospital (neo-Gothic); Johannes Klais organ, 1959, 2 manuals, 56 notes, 15 registers, 17-18 ranks, mechanical key and stop action; case design: Klais; H 17'-1", W 13'-9", D 5'-3"; wood: oak; location: in the rear gallery

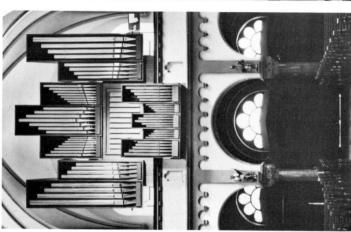

St. Trudpert, Schwarzwald, Germany; St. Trudpert Kloster (c.1930) Johannes Klais organ, 1965,
2 manuals, 56 notes, 25 registers, 32-33 ranks,
mechanical key action, electric stop action;
case design: Klais; H 31'-6", W 15'-9", D 4'-11";
wood: oak; location: in the rear gallery

Bonn - Poppelsdorf, Germany; St. Sebastian (c.
1900), Klais organ, 1963, 3 manuals, 58 notes, 36
registers, 52-53 ranks, mechanical key action, electric stop action; case design: Klais; H 24'-7" W
22', D 4'-8" (RP: H 6'-3", W 8'-2", D 3'-9");
wood: oak; location: in the rear gallery

Himmerod, Eifel, Germany; Cistercienser-Abtei
(Renaissance); Klais organ, 1962, 4 manuals,
58 notes, 55 registers, 79-80 ranks, mechanical
key action, electric stop action; case design:
Klais; H 34'-5", W 23', D 4'-7"; wood: solid oak
stained; location: in the Epistle transept gallery

60

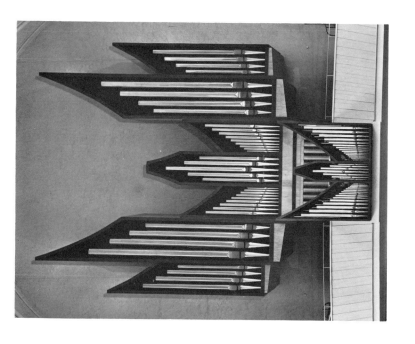

Lisse, Netherlands; Hervormde Kerk (17th Cent.); D. A. Flentrop organ, 1961, 2 manuals, 56 notes, 18 registers, 23 ranks, mechanical key action, mechanical stop action; case design by D. A. Flentrop; height 16'-5", width 17'-5", depth 2'-11"; wood: oak; location: in the rear gallery

Berlin, Germany; Heilandskirche (c.1900), E. Glas, architect; Gerhard Schmid organ, 1962, 3 manuals, 56 notes, 46 registers, 61 ranks, mechanical key action, electric stop action; case design by builder; H 36'-1", W 24'-11", D 2'-7" to 5'-3"; wood: limba and mahogany; location: in the choir

Aabenraa, Denmark; Sct. Nicolai Kirke (old); Marcussen organ, 1956, 3 manuals, 56 notes, 31 registers, 44 ranks, mechanical key and stop action; case design by Kaare Klint, architect; H 20'-3", W 9'-3", D 4'-1"; Pedal: W 3'-10", D 5'; wood: oak; location: the center of the rear

St-Pascal, Quebec, Canada; St-Pascal's Church; Casavant Frères organ, 1964, 3 manuals, 56 notes, 29 registers, 45 ranks, mechanical key and stop action; case design by the builder (Hellmuth Wolff); H 26', W 18'-6"; wood: oak; location: shallow transept at the front

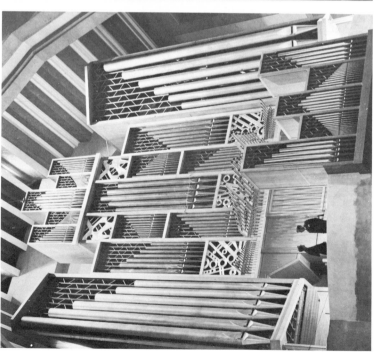

Montreal, Quebec, Canada; Oratory of St. Joseph (contemporary); von Beckerath organ, 1960, 5 manuals, 56 notes, 78 registers, 119 ranks mechanical key action, electric stop action; case design: builder and Bernhard Hopp, architect; H 59'-8", W 42'-10", D 13'; wood: fir; location: in the rear gallery

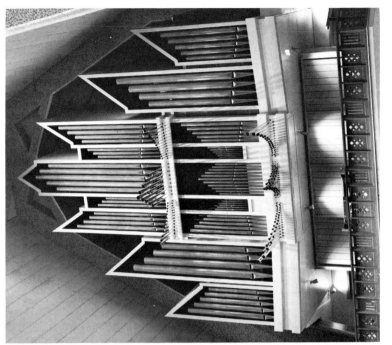

Cap-de-la-Madeleine, Quebec, Canada; Basilique Notre-Dame-du-Cap (1964); Adrien Dufresne, architect; Casavant Frères organ. 1965. 3 manuals, 61 notes, 75 registers, 107 ranks, electro-pneumatic key and stop action; case design by builder; H 49′, W 35′, D 14′, wood: oak; location: rear gallery

Linköping, Sweden; Missionskyrka; organ by Marcussen & Sön, 1962, 2 manuals, 54 notes, 18 registers, 21 ranks, mechanical key action, mechanical stop action; case design by the builder; height 10'-10", width 5'-11", depth 2'-10"; wood: oak; location: on a platform behind the altarpiece

Stockholm, Sweden; S:t Jacobs Kyrka (old); Marcussen & Sön organ, 1960, 2 manuals, 54 notes, 17 registers, 22 ranks, mechanical key and stop action; case design by the builders (Sybrand Zachariassen); H 10'-5", W 5'-11", D 2'-10"; wood: oak; location: at the Epistle side of the nave near front

Vollsjö, Skåne, Sweden; organ built by Olof Hammarberg Orgelbyggare,
Gothenburg, 1962, 2 manuals, 54 notes, about 16 registers and about 18 ranks

Sävedalen, Gothenburg, Sweden; organ built by Olof Hammarberg Orgelbyggare, Gothenburg, 1962, 2 manuals, 54 notes, c. 12 registers and c. 14 ranks

67

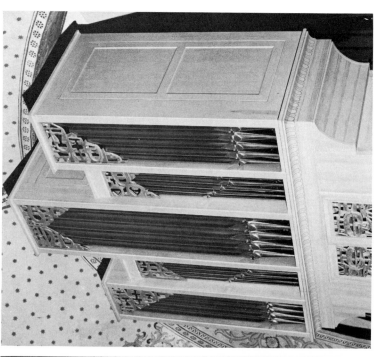

Sorunda, Södermanland, Sweden; Sorunda Kyrka (c.1600); Hammarberg organ, 1964, 2 manuals, 54 notes, 18 registers, 23 ranks, mechanical key action, mechanical stop action; case design by the builder; carving by J. Seldenthuis; height 18'-8", width 11'-6", depth 4'-5"; wood: fir; location: in the gallery

Boston, Massachusetts; New England Conservatory of Music; Hammarberg organ, 1964, 2 manuals, 56 notes, 12 registers, 15 ranks, mechanical key and stop action; case design by the builder, carving by J. Seldenthuis; height 10'-6", width 9'-6", depth 3'-7"; wood: blond Swedish fir

Simrishamn, Skåne, Sweden; Simrishamn Kyrka (c.1200); Hammarberg organ, 1965, 2 manuals, 54 notes, 19 registers, 23 ranks, mechanical key and stop action; case design by the builder, carving by J. Seldenthuis; H. 13'-1", W 10'-6", D 9'-10"; wood: fir; location: in the rear gallery

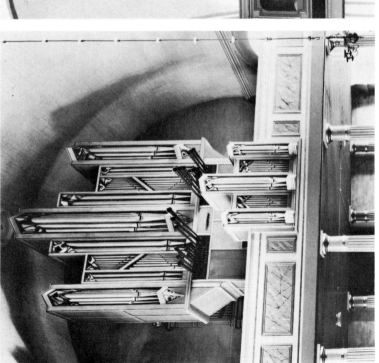

Boda, Dalecarlia, Sweden; Boda Kyrka (c.1800); Hammarberg organ, 1963, 2 manuals, 54 notes, 24 registers, 31 ranks, mechanical key action, mechanical stop action; case design by the builder, carving by J. Seldenthuis H 22'-4", W 13'-1", D 5'-1"; wood: fir; location: in the rear gallery

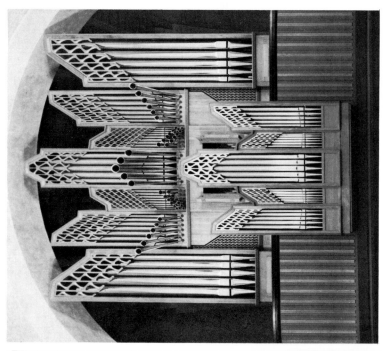

Höganäs, Sweden: Höganäs Kyrka: organ by Marcussen & Sön, 1958, 3 manuals, 29 registers, 39 ranks, mechanical key and stop action; case design by the builder (P. G. Andersen): height 17'-5", width 13'-6", depth 3'-0", Rückpositiv: width 5'-4", depth 2'-4"; location: in the rear gallery

Lund, Sweden: Sct. Peters Klosters Kyrka (old); Marcussen & Sön organ, 1959, 3 manuals, 27 registers, 35 ranks, mechanical key and stop action; case design by the builder (P. G. Andersen): H 16'-11", W 10'-8", D 2'-11"; Rückpositiv: W 4'-8", D 2'-4"; wood: oak; location: in the rear gallery

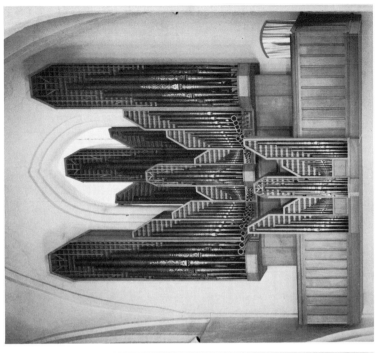

Slagelse, Denmark; St. Mikkels Kirke (old); Marcussen organ, 1961, 3 manuals, 56 notes, 33 registers, 43 ranks, mechanical key action, mechanical (manuals) & electric (Pedal) stop action; case design; builder (P. G. Andersen); H 20'-10", W 14', D 2'-2" to 4'-7"; wood: oak; in the rear gallery

Vordingborg, Denmark; Vor Frue Kirke (old); Marcussen & Sön organ, 1960, 3 manuals, 27 registers, 34 ranks, mechanical key action and mechanical stop action; case design by Marcussen & Sön (P. G. Andersen); height 21'-8", width 17'-11", depth 3'-10"; wood: oak; location: in the rear gallery

Kaufbeuren, Germany; Dreifaltigkeitskirche (Rococo); Gerhard Schmid organ, 1964, 4 manuals, 56 notes, 57 registers, 76 ranks, mechanical key action, electric stop action; case design by the builder; H 26'-3", W 21'-3", D 2' to 5'-10"; location: in the galleries back of the altar

Hildesheim, Germany; St. Andreas (13th Cent.); von Beckerath organ, 1965, 4 manuals, 56 notes, 63 registers, 115 ranks, mechanical key action, electric stop action; case by the builder and Gustav Haake; H 53', W 36'-3", D 15'; wood: pine; location: in the rear gallery

73

Richmond, Virginia; Cannon Memorial Chapel, University of Richmond; von Beckerath organ, 1963, 2 manuals, 26 registers, 38-41 ranks, 56 notes; mechanical key and stop action; case design by the builder; height 27'-7", width 20'-1", depth 6'-3"; wood: oak; location: front wall back of chancel

Bielefeld, Germany; Altstädter Nikolaikirche (14th Cent.), restoration 1954. Bernhard Hopp, architect; von Beckerath organ, 1965, 3 manuals, 56 notes, 48 registers, 70 ranks, mechanical key action, electric stop action; case design: builder & Mr. Hopp; H 36'-3", W 26'-3", D 13'-10"; in the rear gallery

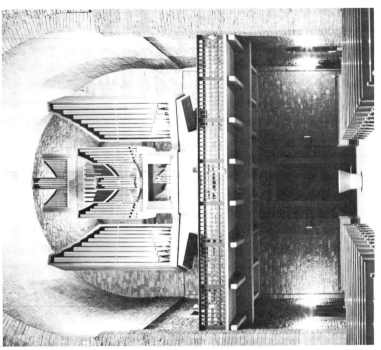

Karlsruhe, Germany: St. Stefan (old), reconstruction by Mr. Rolli, architect; Johannes Klais organ, 1959, 4 manuals, 56 notes, 49 registers, 70-74 ranks, mechanical key action, electric stop action; case design by builder; H 32'-10", W 26'-3", D 6'-7"; wood: oak; location: in the rear gallery

Evanston, Illinois: Alice Millar Chapel, Northwestern University (1964); Jensen & Halstead, architects; Aeolian-Skinner organ, 1964, 4 manuals, 61 notes, 70 registers. 97 ranks, electro-pneumatic action; case design: architects, builder, Grigg Fountain; H 36', W 30', D 12'; location: the rear gallery

Lisbon, Portugal; Cathedral (Romanesque, Gothic, Baroque); Flentrop organ, 1964, 4 manuals, 56 notes, 51 registers, 76 ranks, mechanical key action, electric stop action; case design by the builder; H 40'-2", W 16'-5", D 3'-3"; location: at south wall of the choir near crossing

Bradford, England; Cathedral (13th-15th Cent. & modern); Hill, Norman & Beard organ, 1960. 1 manual (see text), 13 registers, 12-13 ranks, electro-pneumatic action; case design by Sir Edward Maufe, architect; H 34', W 10', D 12'-6"; wood: oak; location: near rear of nave

Middlefart, Denmark; Middlefart Kirke (an early building); organ by Th. Frobenius & Co.,
1962, 3 manuals, 56 notes, 28 registers, about 38 ranks, mechanical key action and mechanical
.stop action; case design by Rolf Graae, architect; wood: oak; location: in the rear gallery

Rönne, Bornholm, Denmark; Rönne Kirke; organ built by Th. Frobenius & Co. in 1961, 3 manuals, 56 notes, 34 registers, approximately 45 ranks, mechanical key action, mechanical stop action; case design by Marinus Andersen, architect; wood: oak; location: in the rear gallery

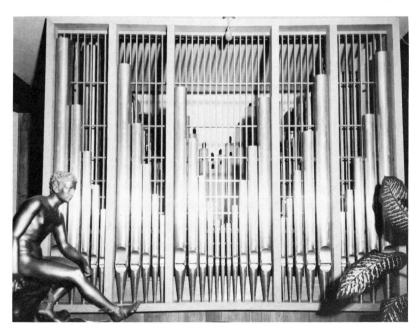

Sulphur, Louisiana; residence of Ted Brooks; organ built by Rubin S. Frels, 1962, 3 manuals, 61 notes, 7 registers, 8 ranks, electric key and stop action; case design by the builder; height 8'-9", width 8'-0", depth 7'-0"; wood: oak with cherry panels on the sides

79

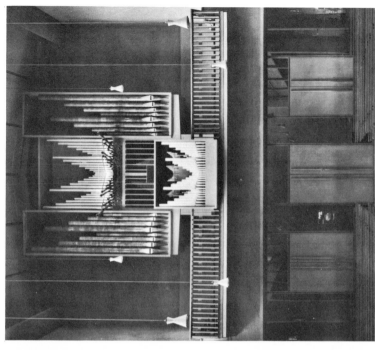

Karlsruhe-Mühlburg, Germany; St. Peter and Paul (c.1950), Werner Groh, architect; Johannes Klais organ, 1961, 3 manuals, 56 notes, 34 registers, 49-50 ranks, mechanical key action, electric stop action; case design: Klais; H 23'-0", W 20'-4", D 3'-11"; wood: spruce; location: in the rear gallery

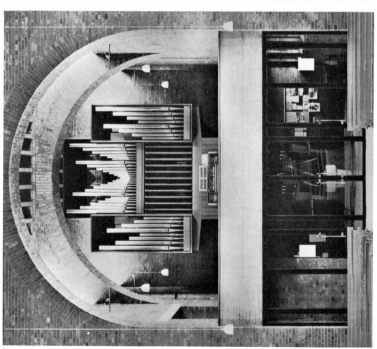

Wesseling-Süd, Germany; St. Marien (c.1955), Mr. Bernhards, architect; Johannes Klais organ, 1962, 2 manuals, 56 notes, 19 registers, 27-28 ranks, mechanical key action, electric stop action; case design by the builder; H 19'-0", W 15'-5", D 3'-7"; wood: oak; location: in the rear gallery

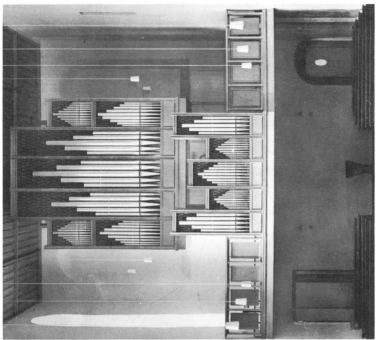

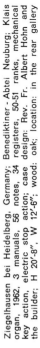

Ziegelhausen bei Heidelberg, Germany; Benediktiner - Abtei Neuburg; Klais organ, 1962, 3 manuals, 56 notes, 34 registers, 50-51 ranks, mechanical key action, electric stop action; case design; Rev. Fr. Albert Hohn and the builder; H 20'-8", W 12'-6"; wood: oak; location: in the rear gallery

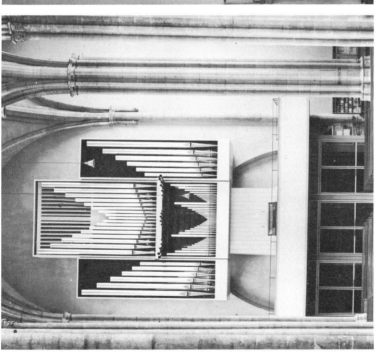

Braunschweig, Germany; St. Aegidien (Gothic); organ by Johannes Klais 1965, 3 manuals, 56 notes, 45 registers, 69 ranks, mechanical key action, electric stop action; case design by Johannes Klais; height 39'-4", width 23'-10", depth 6'-5"; wood: spruce; location: in the rear gallery

Cologne-Lindenthal, Germany; St. Stephanus (1960), Dipl. Ing. Joachim Schürmann, architect; Johannes Klais organ, 1962, 2 manuals, 56 notes, 22 registers, 31-34 ranks, mechanical key action, electric stop action; case design by the builder and Mr. Schürmann; height 33'-0", width 10'-3", depth 5'-9"; wood: larch and Oregon pine; location: in the rear facing the altar

Monheim-Baumberg, Germany; St. Dionysius (c.1955), Dipl. Ing. Rotterdam, architect; Johannes Klais organ, 1961, 2 manuals, 56 notes, 16 registers, 22 ranks, mechanical key action, electric stop action; case design by builder; case design is by Ingenieur Josef von Glatter-Götz; the case-work indicates three manual divisions and Pedal; location: the gallery

Cologne, Germany; Erzbischöfliches Priesterseminar (contemporary); the organ was built by Rieger Orgelbau (Schwarzach, Vorarlberg, Austria) in 1960; the case design is by Ingenieur Josef von Glatter-Götz; the case-work indicates three manual divisions and Pedal; location: the gallery

83

Berlin-Plötzensee, Germany; Regina Martyrum (contemporary), Daombaumeister Schädel, architect; Klais organ, 1963, 3 manuals, 58 notes, 25 registers, 34-36 ranks, mechanical key action, electric stop action; case design by builder; Prestants, front to back 4', 8', 16'; Wood: ash; location: in the rear gallery

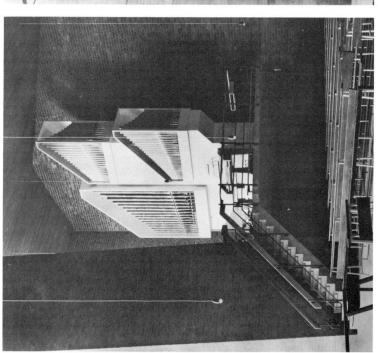

Düsseldorf-Wersten, Germany; St. Maria in den Benden (c.1958) Steffann & Rosiny, architects; Klais organ, 1961, 2 manuals, 56 notes, 15 registers, 20-21 ranks, mechanical key action, electric stop action; case design by the builder: H 18'-1", W 16'-5", D 3'-3"; wood: pine; location: in a corner

Breisach, Germany; St. Stephanus-Münster (Gothic); Johannes Klais organ, 1963, 3 manuals, 56 notes, 36 registers, 50-51 ranks, mechanical key action, electric stop action; case design by builder; H 26'-3", W 24'-7", D 4'-11"; wood: natural oak, pipe shades natural spruce; location: transept gallery

Merzig, Saar; Propstei St. Peter (Romanesque), Baurat Vogel, architect of choir gallery; Klais organ, 1960, 3 manuals, 56 notes, 35 registers, 46-49 ranks, mechanical key action, electric stop action; case design by the builder; H 23'-0", W 21'-4", D 4'-11"; wood: oak; location: in the rear gallery

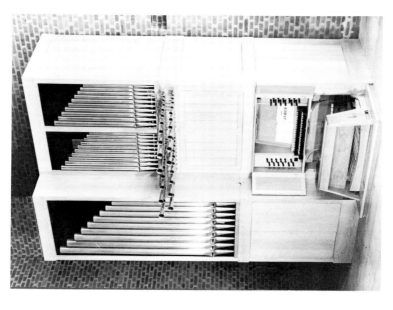

Gothenburg, Sweden; Härlanda Kyrka (1958). Peter v. Celsing, architect; Hammarberg organ, 1960, 2 manuals, 56 notes, 23 registers, 28 ranks, mechanical key and stop action; case design: Nils Hammarberg & architect; H 14'-11", W 8'-6", D 4'-11"; wood: oak; location: at the Epistle side

Mesquite, Texas; St. Stephen Methodist Church (1962), Pratt, Box and Henderson, architects; Sipe-Yarbrough organ, 1962, 2 manuals, 61 notes, 13 registers, 17 ranks, mechanical key and stop action; case design: builder (Rodney Yarbrough) H 13'-11", W 13', D 5'-5"; location: at the back wall

An organ built by the firm of Olof Hammarberg, Gothenburg, Sweden, in 1960; it is a mechanical-action instrument with nineteen ranks; a wood ranks, having natural contrasting stripes is used decoratively; the hinged shutters enclose the key desk; the location is at an end of the rear gallery

Hüttwilen, Switzerland: Reformierte Kirche (1963), Kellermüller & Lanz, architects; Th. Kuhn organ, 1963, 2 manuals, 56 notes, 15 registers, 24-25 ranks, mechanical key action, electric stop action; case design: builder; H 18′, W 14′-5″, D 4′-7″; wood: white fir & oak; location: in the rear gallery

87

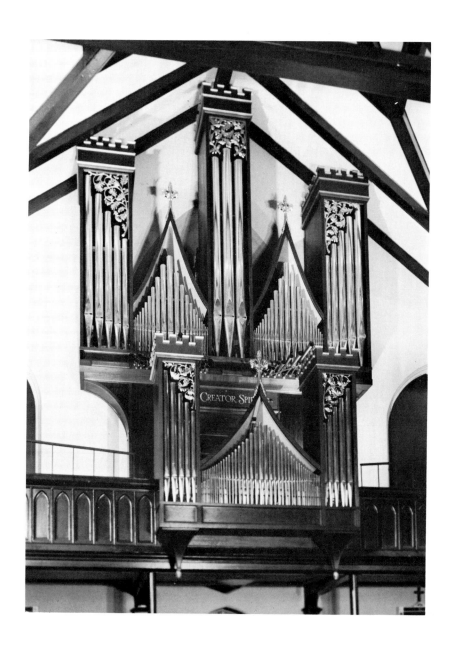

Baltimore, Maryland; Mount Calvary Episcopal Church (1846); organ by Andover Organ Co. (now C. B. Fisk, Inc.),[34] 1961, 2 manuals, 56 notes, 37 registers, 52 ranks, mechanical key and stop action; case design: Charles Fisk and Leo Constantineau; height 21'-4", width 13'-6", depth 2'-4"; Rückpositiv depth 2'-3"; wood: African mahogany; location: in the rear gallery

Locust Valley, Long Island, New York; studio of Richard Lippold, sculptor; organ by the Schlicker Organ Company, Inc., about 1961, 2 manuals, 56 notes, 19 registers, 22-23 ranks, mechanical key action, mechanical stop action; the wire mesh design is by Mr. Lippold; height about 14', width at the base about 6', width at level of the Pedal compartments about 10'-3"

London, England; St. John the Evangelist, Islington (1843): organ by J. W. Walker & Sons, 1963, 3 manuals, 61 notes, 41 registers, 47 ranks, electro-pneumatic action; case design: case design by builder; H 24'-6", W 15', D 10'; Rückpositiv H 9'-6", W 9'-6", D 5'; softwood painted; location: in the rear gallery

London, England; St. Philip's, Kensington (1853), T. Johnson, architect; N. P. Mander organ, 1964, 3 manuals, 61 notes, 68 registers, 52 ranks, electro-pneumatic action; case design by builder; woodwork: mahogany; interior of pipe frames white, edges gold leaf; location: in the rear gallery

St. Paul, Minnesota; Unity Church (1905-T. G. Holyoke), rebuilt 1964, Hammel & Green, architects; Noack organ, 1965, 3 manuals, 56 notes, 31 registers, 42-44 ranks, mechanical key action, electric stop action; case: Fritz Noack & Richard Hammel; H 19', W 20', D 4'; wood: birch; rear gallery

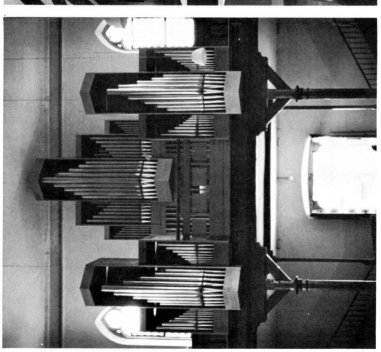

Egg, Vorarlberg, Austria; Roman Catholic Church (older building); organ built by Rieger completed about 1964, mechanical action; the case design is by Ingenieur Josef von Glatter-Götz; the wood is natural oak; there is a detached console just back of the railing; location: in the rear gallery

91

Bjursas, Dalecarlia, Sweden; Bjursas Kyrka; Hammarberg organ, 1961, 2 manuals, 54 notes, 26 registers, 33 ranks, mechanical key and stop action; case design by builder and Erik Lundgren; height 18', width 16'-5", depth 5'-7"; wood: fir; location: in the rear gallery

Schutterwald, Baden, Germany; St. Jacobi (c.1780); Johannes Klais organ, 1964, 3 manuals, 56 notes 35 registers, 50 ranks, mechanical key action, electric stop action; case design: Klais; height 19'-4"; wood: spruce painted white with red trim; location: in the rear gallery

Burgbrohl, Germany; St. Joseph Krankenhaus (1964); Johannes Klais organ, 1965, 2 manuals, 56 notes, 12 registers, 16 ranks, mechanical key action, electric stop action; case design: by the builder; H 17'-7", W 14'-10", D 3'-6" to 4'-3"; wood: oak; location: at the back wall

Nürnberg, Germany; St. Bartholomäus (rebuilt 1956), Gottlieb Schwemmer, architect; Gerhard Schmid organ, 1961, 3 manuals, 56 notes, 39 registers, 53 ranks, mechanical key and electric stop action; case design: O. L. Zimmermann; H 20'-8", W 23'; wood: limba; location: the choir

Wolfville, N.S., Canada; Chapel, Acadia University (1963), Harold E. Wagoner, architect; Casavant organ, 1963, 2 manuals, 56 notes, 20 registers, 28 ranks, all mechanical action; case design: Casavant (Karl Wilhelm); H 17'-1", W 11'-4", D 7'-5"; wood: oak; location: rear gallery

Grand Forks, North Dakota; United Lutheran Church (c.1925); Casavant Frères organ, 1964, 3 manuals, 56 notes, 34 registers, 49 ranks, mechanical key and stop action; case design: Casavant (Karl Wilhelm); H 18', W 28'-3", D 7'; wood: oak and walnut; location: in the rear gallery

Bäckaby, Smaland, Sweden; Bäckaby Kyrka (c.1905); Hammarberg organ, 1961, 2 manuals, 54 notes, 15 registers, 18 ranks, mechanical key and stop action; case design: H. Thavfelin, architect; H 16'-5", W 12'1", D 4'-11"; wood: Swedish fir painted; location: in the rear gallery

Frankfurt, Germany; St. Katharinenkrankenhaus (modern), Giefer & Mäckler, architects; Klais organ, 1963, 2 manuals, 56 notes, 18 registers, 23 ranks, mechanical key and stop action; case: Klais; H 18'-1", W 19'-8", D 3'-11"; wood: cherry; location: in the rear gallery

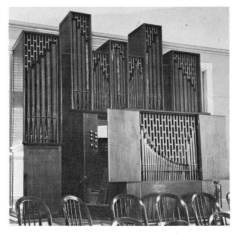

Winston-Salem, North Carolina; Salem College; Flentrop organ, 1957, 2 manuals, 56 notes, 16 registers, 21 ranks, mechanical key and stop action; case design: by the builder; H 10'-9", W 11'-6"; D 2'-2"

Montevallo, Alabama; Alabama College; D. A. Flentrop organ, c.1960, 2 manuals, 56 notes, 13 registers, 15 ranks, mechanical key and stop action; case design: by the builder; H 12'-0", W 12'-6", D 1'-9"

Baden, Switzerland, Methodistenkirche (c.1900); Kuhn organ, 1963, 2 manuals, 56 notes, 11 registers, 13-14 ranks; all mechanical action; case: builder; H 10', W 9', D 5'; wood: white fir; location: in choir room

Kent, Ohio; Kent State University Music Center (1960); Schantz organ, 1960, 2 manuals, 16 registers, 4 ranks (unified), electro-pneumatic action; case design: Schantz; H 12'-3", W 12'-7", D 3'; wood: oak.

FORCED PIPE LENGTHS

❧

There are still organ builders in Europe as well as in England and the United States who erect pipe fences[1] around their products; their condition, I fear, is hopeless.[26] But even among better builders, there are designers who will force the length of Prestants[27] which tends to

[26] That the designers of highly publicized organs built each year in the United States and England and of some on the European continent persist in these enlightened times in placing strange looking pipes of false length where Prestants should be is quite beyond my comprehension. I have come to the conclusion that they must be completely devoid of any esthetic sense, of any knowledge at all of musical or architectural or pipe scales, of any training in design, of any powers of observation, and of any idea whatsoever of what a genuine pipe organ looks like, and that they spent their formative years surrounded by a picket fence and today have a psychotic compulsion to symbolize their fence in each organ front they perpetrate. One has only to turn through the pages of *The Diapason* and *The American Organist* each month to see the crimes that are committed on this side of the Atlantic. The designers of most of the cases illustrated in this volume would consider themselves libelled if these horrors were attributed to them yet their builders unblushingly publicize them. One can only hope that the organs behind these fronts do not sound as atrocious as they look.

A builder sent me a photograph of an organ recently completed by his firm in which there were flats of pipes which decreased in diameter as they increased in length; and one end of a dozen pipes could not be more than three semitones from the other end, and in the same sequence of what would normally be an octave, the scaling would graduate from that of a thin Salicional to a Principal. I received from another builder a picture of an organ completed in 1965 which shows in the front identical sequences of pipes of *eight* identical Salicional 8' registers. (The stop list does not mention them.) If I were cruel, I would quote the builder's laudatory comment on this front. The front of another organ completed this year has *seventy-two* open pipes all of which would speak the same pitch (which appears to be about 8'-C) and, in addition, enough Salicionals of proper length to fence several corrals (pronounced the same as, but not, *chorales*).

This sort of thing was almost universal in America forty years ago for we actually had a generation here then which had grown up without ever having seen an organ inasmuch as they were all hidden in caverns. But where have these Rip Van Winkle organ builders been the last twenty-five years and what will they do when they wake up?

[27] Prestants which have a slot in the back with either a slider or a coil for tuning must be longer than the actual pitch length to allow for the tuning device. Since each Prestant is lengthened in the same ratio, it does not affect the natural appearance of the pipes; it merely makes them appear to have a slightly narrower scale than they actually have. This is not what I mean by forcing. Prestants of false or forced length are those which are extended beyond the necessary length; these false extensions may vary from an inch or two to several feet. The pipes must have openings in the back to keep them from speaking their natural pitch.[1]

damage, if not to spoil, the effect of otherwise commendable case designs. These few comments on the subject are intended to be constructive criticism.

The only excuse for forcing the length of a pipe in any degree would be to make the pipe look right if in its natural length it looked wrong. The ancient Greek architects used corrective measures to make elements of buildings look right. The purpose of entasis, or swelling of columns, was to make the column sides look straight instead of concave. The columns at the corners were set a bit closer to the adjacent columns than the regular intercolumniation of the colonnade simply to make the space look the same as the others. This is also the reason a good typographer will set in a title a little less space between the end letters and adjacent ones than he puts between the interior letters. The corner columns in the Parthenon were made broader than the others so they would not appear to be thinner. The colonnades were designed to lean inward so they would not appear to lean outward. The stylobates were curved upward to the center so they would not appear to sag. Students of architecture know that the Greeks resorted to the use of other corrective refinements. Rembrandt forced his lights and darks not only for dramatic effect but also for reasons of composition in chiaroscuro.

Many more instances where designers have forced dimensions or values just to make elements look right instead of wrong could be cited. It was not until comparatively modern times when archaeological experts were making careful measurements that the tricks of the old Greek architects were discovered—since the temples looked right, there was no reason to question the thicknesses, levels and verticals.

So, if a pipe at its natural length should look shorter than natural, a designer would be justified in adding an increment with cut-out back to make it look right. I do not believe any such situation ever existed. If one should look longer than natural, it obviously could not be made shorter because it would be made sharp. If the designer of an organ case should ever add false length to pipes and should succeed in having them end up looking right, they would never be questioned for no one but he and the pipe maker would ever know the difference. My objection is to those which look false.

In the planning stage of this study, it was my intention not to include in the illustrations any cases in which pipes of forced length were obvious. A few have been included because they have sufficient interest or merit to outweigh that one glaring fault inherited from 19th-Century case design. The most readily apparent examples are in the two center flats in Kings Park Church, Glasgow (37), the center tower in Our Lady of Mount Carmel, Yonkers (39), St. Stephan, Karlsruhe (75), the corner towers in Bradford Cathedral (77), in Härlanda (86), in the organ in the unidentified Swedish church (87), in

St. John the Evangelist, London (90), in the upper groups of pipes in Burgbrohl (93) and in the Brustwerk of Bäckaby Church (95). The objectionable artificial appearance of more than half these cases could be eliminated merely by cutting the Prestants with forced length down to their natural lengths. The others would require a bit of additional study.

When the designer forces the lengths of Prestants, he invariably loses more than he gains. Symmetry which is obviously forced always looks bad. To have both pipe tops and pipe mouths in straight lines always looks false. Groups of pipes in which the individual pipes do not decrease in length in proper ratio to their reduction in scale or diameter always look fraudulent. The designer can never go wrong with Prestants if he keeps them to their natural lengths. He cannot help but go wrong if he makes them longer than their speaking lengths.

A case which could have been ruined by forcing pipe lengths is that of the Flentrop organ in St. Andrew's Church (59) in Malmö; it is an unusual one which could have been extremely dull if it had not been done by an expert designer. It is a work-principle organ with ten registers in each manual division and eleven in the Pedal; the Principal of the Brustwerk is at 2', the Rückpositiv shows its Prestant 4', the Hauptwerk its Prestant 8', and the Pedal its Prestant 16' in the divided compartments. It is an excellent and subtle design and its excellence is the result of its subtleties.

The composition in its basic concept is a simple one of verticals and diagonals. The obvious treatment of this idea would be to make the tops of the Hauptwerk and Pedal compartments parallel, to force the line of the pipe tops into a rigid parallel with the compartment tops and to force an absolute symmetry between the pipes on one side and those on the other. Some organ builders would even keep the line of mouths horizontal by extreme false lengths on the pipes. This designer was too knowing to let himself fall into any of those traps.

An element of the concept is the filling of the openings with Prestants. To maintain a balance between the dark voids above the pipes of one side and those of the other, all the feet on the C-sharp side were made longer than those of the C side. Consequently, the three lines of pipe mouths on the right are slightly higher than the corresponding lines on the left. The eye is satisfied by the rigid symmetry of the case structure; the conscious avoidance of rigid symmetry in the Prestants makes the organ look as genuine as it is.

SILHOUETTE AND FACADE PATTERN

The first impression one receives of an organ when he enters a church, especially if it is a dimly lighted one, is its silhouette. It follows that the designer should study the silhouette to make certain that it has satisfying proportions. Since the façade pattern and the silhouette are integrally related, they must be studied together. The designer can begin with either one, deciding arbitrarily which it will be; if the starting point is the façade pattern, it will govern the silhouette. On the other hand, the silhouette as a point of departure will only influence the arrangement of the pipes as there is more latitude there. The design of the lateral cross section, and hence the silhouette, is sometimes of necessity influenced by ceiling heights and contours.

It will be seen in the illustrations that the façade patterns of contemporary cases range from simple undivided openings containing a single flat through three-part and five-part arrangements up to multipartite patterns. Usually and logically, the smallest organs have the simplest façades and the largest the most complex.

There are more organ cases with five-part façades—three towers and two flats—than there are with any other one composition.[28] For simplifying identification, I shall call those having the center tower lower than the side towers the *Totentanz* type because the old organ in the Totentanz Chapel[4] of the Marienkirche in Lübeck had this silhouette. The old rear gallery[4] organ in the same church had a center tower higher than the side towers but for the sake of avoiding confusion, I shall call this the *Salamanca* type since the organ in the old Cathedral[4] in Salamanca also had this arrangement of towers and flats.[29] As the cases illustrated are discussed, other place names will be used for convenience in identifying types.

The organs in St. Eusebiuskerk (42) in Arnhem and in St. Maria Königin (43) in Bodenwerder are worthy of comparison. Each is the Totentanz type and although their proportions are similar they are different in that the super-structure of the van Vulpen organ is wider than that of the Klais. The additional width of the first is a result of its wider flats; the towers of both organs are approximately the same since each tower contains five Prestant pipes. Those in St. Eusebius are, as one would expect, the Prestant 8′ of the Hauptwerk but those

[28] This statement in no way implies that most cases have five-part facades; they definitely do not.

[29] There are not regional implications at all in these names; they are chosen merely for convenience. It would be awkward to call the second the *Lübeck Marienkirche rear gallery* type.

in St. Maria Königin are the Principalbass 8′ of the Pedal; the Haupt-werk Principal there is at 4′. This case deviates from tradition slightly (as do some others in the illustrations) in that there are no more pipes in the flats than in the towers. Other than the difference in width of the flats of the two cases, their silhouettes are more or less the same except for the very deep splays at the impost in the van Vulpen case; they are unusual in that they run the full height of the Brustwerk.

The design of both these cases is strictly contemporary in con-cept; there is no semblance of ornamental motifs from any previous period. They are completely devoid of cornices or other decorative mouldings. One is in a Gothic church probably built when Arnhem was a Hanseatic town and the other is in a contemporary structure, yet each is in harmony with its architectural environment.

At Arnhem, the principal unifying element between Gothic and contemporary is in the pipe shades which are from the atelier of J. Seldenthuis and J. G. J. A. ten Berge of Maarssen, Netherlands. Good ornament which does not borrow heavily from motifs of the past is difficult to achieve. These pipe shades merit examination. Horizontal, vertical and diagonal lines in geometric order are superimposed upon free but balanced ornamental elements resulting in a coloristic pat-tern of voids and solids. The shades are symmetrical about the vertical axis of the case and, in the towers, projections at each pipe give one the impression at first glance that some pipes have been given false lengths to force a rigid symmetry but the tops of the natural-length tin pipes gleam through the openings to prove there is no such fool-ishness here.

The organ in Bodenwerder is stark in its simplicity. There is no trace of ornament or applied color. It depends for its effect entirely upon the form of the casework, the pattern of the pipes and the tex-ture and local color of the materials. It, too, is in harmony with its architectural environment.

It is my contention that these two organs could be exchanged and neither organ and neither building would suffer visually. There would be a difference, however, for where there is now blend in each instance, by an exchange, contrast would be introduced in each in-stance. There would be contrast but not incongruity.

SALAMANCA AND SORO TYPES

⟨❧⟩

The van Vulpen organ in the Pauluskerk in The Hague (44) is one of fine proportions and great dignity. There is a subtle and refined use of color; the cavetto cornices, painted white, pick up the theme of the four columns and the cantilevered slab of the gallery. A rich red, used on parts of the pipe shades and inside the case, is shown in its full brilliance only as an edging around the inside surfaces of the openings. The panels of the Hauptwerk toeboards are blue. The Hauptwerk case is of the Salamanca type and while the Rückpositiv repeats the general form, it has a proportionately wider center tower and narrower flats containing double Prestants. This diversity between the two cases adds to the variety of elements and thus makes a more lively contrast between the organ and its somewhat austere background.

A Rieger organ, also of the Salamanca type, is in a "swallow's nest" high on the south wall of the choir of the Minster in Ulm (45). The pointed side towers of the main case and the tower of the three-part Rückpositiv are unifying elements between the two cases, as are the pipe shades when all are in place. This handsome organ of contemporary design is a fitting addition to the old Gothic building.

Of the four cases illustrated on pages 38 and 39, those in Stamford, Connecticut, and in Tyler, Texas, are of the Salamanca type and that in Yonkers, New York, and the Hauptwerk of the one in Batesville, Arkansas, are variations of it. Each of the four is a two-manual instrument; as can be seen, two have the second division in a Rückpositiv case and two have it in the Brust.

The Batesville church dates from 1957. It is designed in the simplest manifestation of the Georgian Colonial style. In the case of most modern buildings which are categorized as of some historic style, it is obvious to schooled architects that the designer was only floundering in ignorance of the style in which he thought he was working. This little building was designed with a knowing eye. It is a proper foil for the highly stylized and ornate organ case. While the copper pipes commonly used by Mr. Flentrop and other builders have the manufactured variegated matte patina referred to elsewhere, these Prestants are of burnished copper; they reflect the light from the multiplicity of lamps in the candelabra and gleam with the warmth and vitality of Williamsburg brass candlesticks. The Rückpositiv repeats exactly the pattern composition of the Hauptwerk, a traditional practice which plays a part in giving unity to the whole case composition. The diagonal toeboards in the flats of the two cases are strongly

Dutch in character yet they do not detract from the feeling of architectural affinity between the organ case and the building. The pipe shades and the decoration between the Pedal and Hauptwerk towers, rococo in quality, and the ornamental brackets beneath the towers add to the richness of the case. The trumpetting *putti* suggest that this is an instrument for joyous worship.

The organ in St. Francis' Episcopal Church in Stamford, built in 1963 by Van Zoeren, Henderson & Steinkampf, has a case strictly in the contemporary style and yet it is quite at home in its environment. Here again the Rückpositiv case reflects that of the Hauptwerk; the flutes in the Rückpositiv façade are a necessary compromise because there is no Principal on the chest in this case. A Prestant 4' is in the Hauptwerk; front pipes of both cases are of tin. Their silvery color is enhanced by the blue of the painted interior surfaces of the cases.

The Sipe organ of 1965 in the Presbyterian Chapel in Tyler, Texas, was designed for a building of 1950 having Georgian details such as the entablature capping the walls. The designer of the case, by judicious use of form, color and materials, has succeeded very well in making the organ a handsome addition to the church interior. The Honduras mahogany of the key desk, the turned stop knobs and the cornices carries the mahogany color of the backs and trim of the pews into the chancel where it is needed. The dark cornices give vigor and accent, yet do not impair the inherent dignity of the design. No little part of the interest of this case lies in the lines of the pipe mouths. The tin Prestants are surmounted by pipe shades which are simple wooden grilles gilded. The birch case is painted an off-white. The key desk will be screened from the congregation by a low reredos behind the communion table.

The Delaware Organ Company's case in Yonkers has an almost primitive quality which is appealing. The wide overhang of the Hauptwerk and the cavetto brackets are among the many good points which make one willing to overlook the much too short feet of the outside pipes of the center tower and the somewhat wide spaces between the pipes. The illustration, by not showing its full height, does not do this handsome case justice.

All four of these organ cases are successful solutions to the individual problem.

The main cases of the organ in St. Remigius, Bonn (52), and the Mariehöj Kirke, Silkeborg (53), are essentially Salamanca types set between cantilevered Pedal towers. They are almost awesome in their simple monumentality. Each has a striking silhouette adapted to a large window behind and each depends for much of its effect upon the rugged visible structural members.

The Marcussen organ in the Vestsidens Kirke in Fredrikstad (57), notwithstanding the differences in Prestant patterns, is strongly remindful of the late 15th-Century case in Perpignan.[4] Its Rückpositiv is unusual in that it is not set into the gallery rail but has room for an organist's bench between the case and the rail. A manual, music rack and stop knobs may be seen in the illustration. This arrangement is mainly for use during choir practice but it also facilitates the use of the Rückpositiv as a continuo organ with orchestra.[30]

It was pointed out in my earlier study that the façade pattern of the magnificent old case in Sorö[4] was essentially that of the organ in the rear gallery of the Jakobikirche[4] in Lübeck, and that the Marcussen organ of 1949 in the Oskarskirken[4] in Stockholm was even more closely patterned after the Lübeck composition. Even though the Jakobikirche case is the prototype, to avoid ambiguity in that there is another old organ in that church, I prefer to designate this façade pattern as the Sorö type.

Both the Ahrend & Brunzema organ of 1959 in the Zorgvlietkerk (49) in Scheveningen and the van Vulpen instrument of 1960 in the Reformed Church (48) in Nieuwendijk are of the Sorö type. Each of these façades has only a single tier of pipes in the outside flats while the prototype has two tiers and in the Nieuwendijk organ the double Prestants of the inside flats follow the sequence of Sorö but those in the Zorgvlietkerk have the longest pipe in the center. The observer will see other minor variations such as the lack of a toeboard between the doubles in Scheveningen. The Rückpositiv in Nieuwendijk is a miniature of the Hauptwerk façade; that in Scheveningen is a simple five-part composition.

The case in Scheveningen is of oak painted in two shades of blue. The dark areas in the photograph are a rich deep blue; the light areas are pale blue. The pipe shades are gold and the Trumpets and the embossed pipe in each flat and tower are of gold color, probably gold leaf; all other pipes are of the natural tin color.

The Nieuwendijk case is of Oregon pine painted red and green; the pipe shades are oak. The Spanish Trumpets are surfaced with gold leaf. It is worthy of note that the Rückpositiv case is wholly free-standing and that this has been accomplished by introducing completely new segments of railing between it and the old balcony rail.

The Hauptwerk case of the Leeflang organ in the Immanuëlkerk (51) in Delft is almost a duplicate of the same builder's case in the

---

[30] Mr. S. J. Zachariassen of Marcussen & Sön has informed me that there are such individual manuals in the Haderslev Domkirke,[4] the Sorö Klosterkirke[4] and the Eliaskirke in Copenhagen. In the first, it is in the gallery under the organ gallery and has pneumatic action; in the second, it is behind the organ and has mechanical action to the Rückpositiv; and in the third, it is behind the organ and has mechanical action to the Swell division. There undoubtedly are other organs in Europe with such arrangements. There are, of course, somewhat similar examples in the United States such as the individual keyboard on the Reuter rear-gallery positiv[4] in St. Alban's Episcopal Church in Waco, Texas.

Pniëlkerk (50) in Apeldoorn. They are akin to the two cases just mentioned in that they have divided compartments between center and side towers but they have the Totentanz silhouette while those in Nieuwendijk and Scheveningen have the Salamanca silhouette. Perhaps the most striking difference between the two Leeflang cases, aside from the pipe shades, is in the color and texture of the Prestants.

SOME SUBSTYLES

❧

An early Italian Renaissance pipe pattern is that of the organs[4] in San Giovannino dei Cavallieri in Florence and on the Epistle side in San Stefano in Pisa. The Hauptwerk cases of the Klais organs in the Neuburg Benedictine Abbey (81), Ziegelhausen near Heidelberg, and St. Jacobi (92), Schutterwald, demonstrate the effectiveness of this pattern in contemporary design.

The Rückpositivs, each containing twelve ranks, are well related to the other casework. That in Ziegelhausen is a flattened Totentanz type which depends upon pipe groupings to tie it to the main case. Those of the side towers, even though double bialternates instead of triple bialternates, relate to the Hauptwerk towers; that of the center tower, even though in simple bialternate arrangement instead of double bialternate, relates to the lower flats of the main case; and those of the flats duplicate the upper flats of the main case.

The Rückpositiv in Schutterwald is more unusual and bears a more interesting relationship to the Hauptwerk. Its three flats, like the three towers of the Hauptwerk, are in triple bialternate arrangement, which makes of them miniature towers of pipes reflecting those of the Hauptwerk. Placing the longest pipes of the Prestant 4' in side towers makes the case top an inversion of that of the Hauptwerk. The pattern of each Rückpositiv side tower with its adjoining flat is picked up in the corresponding detached Pedal tower.

As in the Italian prototypes, the pipe mouths in each individual division case of these German organs are maintained in a single line. This is an important feature in the design of both organs; at Schutterwald, it is a unifying element between Hauptwerk and Pedal cases.

It has been pointed out previously that early Italian designers exaggerated the intervals between tops of adjacent Prestants by alternating them among three tower groupings and that the Danish firm of Th. Frobenius had developed this idea by alternating Prestants in several adjoining compartments. By sloping the line of the pipe mouths, the intervals can be decreased as in the Frederiksberg Hospital organ[4] in Copenhagen and the one in Kalvehave, Denmark,[4] or there can be extreme intervals as in the church in Tranebjerg[4] on the island of Samsö. The Tranebjerg effect is the result of alternating the pipes in six groupings while keeping the mouths in line. In the Hauptwerk at Middlefart (78), there are eight groupings (counting the center bialternate tower as two single alternates) and so the intervals would have been even more extreme than those in Tranebjerg had the mouths been kept in line. The Frobenius variations on this theme, although never stereotyped, became so much an individual stylization that they could easily be identified as Frobenius designs. The idea now has been picked up by so many builders that we can refer to it only as the Frobenius style. The Tranebjerg Prestant pattern has been effectively adapted to the case (79) of a small residence organ by Rubin Frels.

Alternates of four groups give the effect shown in the Hauptwerk cases of the Frobenius organ (79) in Rönne[31] and the Klais organs (80) in St. Marien, Wesseling-Süd, and St. Peter and St. Paul, Karlsruhe-Mühlburg. Of these three, only the Frobenius design has a horizontal line of mouths.

The four Klais organs on page 58 obviously are of the same individual style. The Hauptwerk cases at Remscheid and Dernbach are simple three-part compositions; those in Gleuel and Gladbeck are modifications of the Salamanca type. The style character is derived not only from the sloping sides and truncated tops of the cases but also from the lack of vertical supports between towers and flats. Thus, at Gladbeck the Rückpositiv has the latter characteristic in common with the cases of the other divisions so that there is a stylistic tie even though the case is only a simple rectangular box. It does not have, however, the complete stylistic unity with the other three cases which the Rückpositiv in Gleuel has.

The four Flentrop designs on pages 40 and 41 likewise are a definite substyle which depends upon angularity for its distinguishing character. The Hauptwerk cases in Hamburg and Klundert are modifications of the Totentanz type; the Rückpositiv at Klundert repeats the design of the larger case. Although there are more horizontals in the organ in Seattle and it is monumental in scale, it is in this stylistic group. Other Flentrop organs in the same category are one of 1958 in the Nederlands Hervormde Opstandingskerk in Den Helder, Netherlands, and one of 1963 in the Roman Catholic Church in Suffisant, Curaçao; both have two-manuals.

A stylization somewhat more extreme in angularity than the Flentrops (and earlier in the case at Amersfoort) is evident in the van Vulpen organs,[18] built in 1956 and 1958 respectively, in the Bergkerk in Amersfoort and the Opstandingskerk in Eindhoven. Each has a Rückpositiv and there is a detached Pedal tower at Eindhoven; in the five individual division cases there is not a horizontal above the toeboards. The tops of all towers and flats and the lines formed by the

---

[31] The photograph is confusing. Apparently the Brustwerk case is in front of the Hauptwerk; the hiding of the Hauptwerk pipe feet is unfortunate. Another unfortunate feature is that the Prestant 16′ pipes stand in front of the Pedal cases. This obviously was caused by the restrictions of the building; one wonders if a Principal 16′ was really needed in a building so small.

tops and mouths of the pipes are all sloping.[32] Both of these cases are of good design.

Perhaps the seed of the ideas for casework in these Flentrop and van Vulpen organs was in the Flentrop organ[4] of 1954 in the Doopsgezinde Kerk in Rotterdam. There is not even a horizontal toeboard in that organ.

The casework of the new organ by Casavant Frères in the Basilique Notre-Dame-du-Cap (65) in Cap-de-la-Madeleine bears a stylistic kinship to these Dutch organs.

Another Flentrop substyle depending on angularity may be seen in the organs in Leidschendam (59), Malmö (59) and Alabama College (96). Earlier Flentrop organs in the same substyle, dating from 1958 and 1959 respectively, are those in the Nederlands Hervormde Paaskerk in Zaandam and in the Gereformeerd Fonteinkerk in Voorburg. The first has one manual[33] and an independent Pedal with nine registers and twelve ranks in the two divisions; the second is a two-manual organ of twenty-two registers and thirty-two ranks.

It is apparent in the illustrations that the von Beckerath cases in the Oratory of St. Joseph (64) in Montreal, St. Andreas (73) in Hildesheim and the Altstädter Nicolaikirche (74) in Bielefeld that this builder uses splays in vertical planes. This is true also of his five-division organ of 1962 in St. Paul's Cathedral, Pittsburgh, Pennsylvania. This characteristic has in recent years become so much a von Beckerath stylization that it is a mark of identification for his later work.

The three Gress-Miles organs on page 36 show an individual stylization in Hauptwerk-Brustwerk relationship, cantilevered overhangs of the Hauptwerk towers (no brackets are needed for there are no roller-boards), shutters for and center posts in Brustwerk openings, the same kind of panelling on the sides of the case and a total lack of pipe shades and applied ornament. Stereotyping is avoided by the variety of lines of pipe mouths and by changing from the Sion type of the first two Hauptwerk façade patterns to the Totentanz type in the last; the two Sion types are differentiated by the sloping and raised toeboards of the flat in the Woodlawn organ.

Should the builders wish to continue in this style, other woods than walnut and some use of applied color would greatly enlarge their possibilities for variety, and without abandoning this stylistic direction, pipe shades and some ornament could be introduced.

The Marcussen cases designed by P. G. Anderson (56, 70, 71) show a personalized style. The Hauptwerk case, with its matching

---

[32] A letter dated 17 September 1965 from the Gebr. van Vulpen states that they do not intend to build any more cases with sloping tops.

[33] No one-manual organ cases are illustrated because they will be treated in detail in *The Modern One-Manual Organ* now in preparation by George L. Bozeman, Jr., and the author.

Rückpositiv, of the organ in the Höganäs Kirke (70) is adapted from the earlier two-manual Marcussen organ in Glostrup, Denmark.[4]

The Casavant organ in the Sanctuaire Marie-Reine-des-Coeurs (33) in Montreal is an example of a case motif derived directly from a structural feature of the building. When the designer takes this approach, he must know what he is doing because it requires both skill and study to make it come off with the success of this one. This striking case depends for much of its effect upon the arrangement of the Prestants in systems of alternates and the feeling of a simple heavy beam supporting the superstructure of the main case.

DESIGNING IN HISTORIC STYLES

❧

When a new organ is to be designed to go into a building of another time, the question arises as to whether the case shall be designed in the style of the building or in what we are pleased to call the contemporary style. If it is for a new building which is designed in a historical style (or what the designer thinks is one), should the organ case comply stylistically with its environment?

It is my firm opinion that in both architecture and case design, we should work within the modes of expression of our time. Not only is this opinion supported by history but also by many of the organs illustrated which are in buildings dating all the way from a generation or two ago to centuries ago. This does not preclude the designer from borrowing from the past just as Frank Lloyd Wright borrowed from the architecture of ancient Egypt.

But designers (unless coerced by employers or church committees) are free to do as they please which is a good thing, for freedom of design is akin to freedom of speech. The only rules they cannot violate with impunity (other than from the sneers and jeers of their peers) are the laws of statics.

Since he is free, the designer who is designing for an old building can even go back of its period to one earlier. To stay within the period, the designer of the case at Mount Calvary[34] in Baltimore (88) would probably have gone to "prickly Gothic" examples for inspiration. Instead, he jumped across the centuries to the Gothic. I had recognized the Rückpositiv as being of the Sion type and had supposed that the Hauptwerk was inspired by the case in St. Valentin[4] in Kiedrich but was informed by Mr. Constantineau, the principal designer, that the big case in Amiens Cathedral[4] was the inspiration. The Mount Calvary silhouette and architectural scale suggest Kiedrich. Identification of the sources of inspiration for any of the cases

---

[34] When this organ was built, Charles B. Fisk was president of the Andover Organ Company in Methuen, Massachusetts. Now Mr. Fisk heads the firm of Charles B. Fisk, Inc., in Gloucester, Massachusetts, and Leo Constantineau is president of the Andover Organ Company. This case is of special interest to me because I saw it under construction in Methuen when I made a visit there in the fall of 1960. In reply to a request for information from me, Mr. Constantineau wrote, "Although this case design is based on traditional Gothic models, I sought to make it a distillation of the Gothic idea and at the same time impart a simplicity to the decoration and a cleanness to the line, typical in spirit of early American cabinet making and architecture." I think he succeeded in accomplishing his goal. Arthur Howes and D. A. Flentrop consulted with Mr. Fisk in the planning of this organ.

illustrated is only of academic interest; it serves only to show the student of design how elements of old works are transposed, translated and transformed into the new.

When I was a student of architecture, all students attending a school affiliated with the Beaux-Arts Institute were periodically required to do an archaeological problem, commonly termed an *archaeo*, in a particular specified style. While I do not advocate making an archaeo out of designing a modern organ case, I can appreciate one well done and I think no one versed in case design could justly say the Mount Calvary case was not well done. It is beautiful in both concept and execution.

The case is of African mahogany with a finish of oil followed by a sealer. The pipe shades, finials and horizontal edges of the crenelations are gilded. The interior is blue which shows above the tops of the tin pipes in the flats. The colors are rich and impressive.

A particularly interesting fact about the construction of this case is that Mr. Constantineau not only designed the oak leaf shades and the finials but also carved most of the shades himself. The finials were done by a professional woodcarver from Mr. Constantineau's clay model. Such craftsmanship is rare in America today.

For the case of his new organ in the Cathedral in Lisbon (76), Mr. Flentrop has gone for inspiration to a period earlier than that of the organ which it replaced. Where there was a mid-18th-Century rococo-baroque case,[4] there is now a tall handsome case done in the manner of the Renaissance of the 17th Century.

Some designers, while allowing their cases to be frankly contemporary, will tie them into the environment of an earlier period by the simplest of elements. In Trinity Church, Kaufbeuren (72), the curved members, changing in thickness, of the pipe shades help blend the case with the rococo interior. In Lisse (61), the curved moulded tops of the towers are the blending details. In Bäckaby (95), the panels and the rounded tops tie the modern case to the older architecture.

111

ART IN SIMPLICITY

The Klais organ case in St. Stephanus (82) in Cologne-Linden-thal is probably unique.[35] The placing of three chests, one above an-other, has been done time and again but with flanking Pedal towers or with Hauptwerk towers embracing the Oberwerk and often with a Rückpositiv in front so that the resulting composition was nothing like this. A Klais electric-action organ of 1956 in the Church of Maria Empfängnis in Düsseldorf has a Positiv division directly above the Pedal, and the Hauptwerk is at the top directly over the positiv. The case, incomplete because there is no top, is of glass. The concept is different from this in St. Stephanus. The nearest approach to it, so far as I know, is the earlier McManis mechanical-action instrument of 1960 in St. John's Unitarian Church in Cincinnati; its chests are placed in the same relationship to one another: the Swell at the bottom, the Great next above it and the Pedal on top. While there are parallels between these two organs, the Great and Pedal of the McManis are not encased and their chests have different pipe sequences so that in spite of the similarities the overall effect is different.[36]

From front to back, the registers on the Swell windchest in St. Stephanus are Gamba 8', Principal 4', Gedackt 8', Waldflöte 2', Lari-got 1 1/3', Sesquialter II-III, Scharff IV, Regal 8'. Those of the

[35] When I wrote to Mr. Hans Gerd Klais, requesting additional information on this organ, he kindly sent me a print of the working drawings which has enabled me to give rather complete data on it.

[36] The St. Johns Church organ is supported by two exposed steel columns, one on each side, and by the rear wall of the church. The chests are 8', 14' and 22' above the floor as compared to 10'-3", 16'-6" and 22'-3" in St. Stephanus. The pipes of the Great are planted chromatically on the windchest and those of the Pedal are arranged in sequences of 12-13-11-14-10-15-9-16 etc. so that the pipes of the 12-1 octave of the Quintaton 16' generally follow the slope of the shed roof about two feet above them; all three divisions in St. Stephanus have M-chests. At St. John's, the trackers to the Great are exposed to view in front of the Swell box; those to the Pedal may be seen back of the Great and the Pedal rollerboard is visible just under the Pedal chest. As in St. Stephanus, the front pipes of the Great, a Spitzprincipal 8', extend above the Pedal chest at the bass end. In resources, it is a smaller organ, having 13 registers and 15 ranks. It, too, has electrically-controlled stop action. Both buildings were completed in 1960, and just as there was collaboration between organ builder and architect at St. Stephanus, so here Charles McManis and the architect, John M. Garber, of Garber, Tweddell & Wheeler, worked together. I doubt if those responsible for the St. Stephanus organ knew of the existence of the St. John's organ; if they did not, these analogies are all the more interesting. The only reason this Mc-Manis organ is not illustrated is that it is unencased and my subject is limited to contemporary cases; there is a photo in *The Diapason* for September 1, 1960.

Hauptwerk, in the same order, are: Spanische Trompete 8', Principal 8', Rohrflöte 8', Oktav 4', Holztraverse 4', Nasard 2 2/3', Superoktav 2', Dulcian 16', Mixtur IV-VI. From the front, the Pedal registers are: Offenbass 8', Subbass 16', Holzprincipal 4', Rauschpfeife III, Lieblich Posaune 16'.

The blower is not in the pedestal as one might think but in the space above the pedestal and under the Swell windchest at the right end of the main reservoir. There are access doors to this space both in the floor of the Swell platform and the soffit of the case overhang. The Swell shades are Plexiglas jalousies. The ends of the tuner's catwalks at each windchest level can be seen in the illustration.

The entire organ is supported on two large steel channel columns just inside the back of the case and set in to lateral channels of the same section which extend to the front of the pedestal and are set in a concrete slab at floor level. Connecting the forward end of these beams with the columns at the top of the pedestal are steel knee braces. Platforms for the main reservoir and blower, the three windchests and the three catwalks are cantilevered from the two columns. There are ample steel cross braces between the columns.

The pedestal is only 3'-7" by 5'-6" and the whole organ occupies a mere 5'-6" by 8'-8" of floor area. There is headroom of about eight feet under the soffit of the case. The height of the case above the pedestal is 25'-1".

This clean, unadorned tower is a stunning design. Aside from the pipes, which are the chief essential of every organ case façade, it borrows nothing from the historic periods. It says nothing of the past: no condemnation, no ridicule, no homage. It speaks only of today and to the future.

The novice at case design should beware of plain rectangular boxes such as that in St. Stephanus for it takes a designer with a practiced eye and an excellent sense of proportion to make it successful. In the Burgbrohl Hospital (93), a box has been made interesting by the arrangement of the pipes in two sets of triple bialternates with the small groups set on diagonal toeboards. The appearance of this organ would be improved if the forced pipes in the upper groups were cut to their true length. It is never too late to cut pipes down to size.

STOCK DESIGNS

℮∾℮

A number of European builders have one or more stock designs for small mechanical-action organs just as some American builders have a stock unit organ. Some of the European casework is just as wretched as many of the atrocities produced on this side of the Atlantic. Some is of good design but becomes stereotyped from repetition. The firm of Marcussen & Sön has produced fifteen or more small two-manual instruments which are essentially the same but which have variations in case design. Two examples are illustrated on page 66. The so-called "Sweelinck organ"[4] of 1953 in the radio station in Hilversum is another of them; at first glance, it appears to be identical with that in the Jakobs Kyrka, Stockholm, but where the Stockholm case has pipe shades of delicate entertwined vines which grow out of the uprights of the case and support birds taking wing, the pipe shades of the Hilversum example are branches of leaves and flowers which have a more regular pattern of voids and solids than those in Stockholm. Also, the stop knobs are different.

The organs (66) in Stockholm and the Missionskyrka in Linköping afford an excellent lesson in case design. The first has a developed projecting cornice of decorative mouldings; the second has none at all. The first has decorative mouldings at the impost; the second has none. The first has cyma reversa impost brackets; those of the second are simple splays. The two upper flats of the first are in an "A-A" arrangement; those of the second are in an "M" arrangement. The pipe shades of the first are intricate floral and bird forms placed in front of the plane of the pipes; those of the second are narrow vertical strips (stressing verticality) with lozenges between set behind the plane of the pipes. The Brustwerk of the first has reeds in Prestant position with pipe shades; that of the second is open. The first has shutters to enclose the entire superstructure; the second has them only for the Brust. The cornice of the first stresses the horizontal; the vertical members of the second, by projecting above the top, stress verticality. The stop knobs of the first are black; those of the second are faced with white. The pipes of the first have round lips; those of the second pointed ones.

These are the elements which give cases quite distinct in spirit to two organs which basically are identical. Each design is extraordinarily good. A remarkable aspect is that this has been done with the same materials having the same local color. Each case is of natural oak and the Prestants of each are of tin. The distinction is in the form of the details. Stain could have been applied to one, or wood of another color could have been used, or colors could have been applied to the pipe shades of one, or Prestants of copper could have been used in one, or shutters could have been decorated. Fifteen more of this model could be produced without exhausting the possibilities for variety of case design.

ASYMMETRICAL CASES

Contemporary design in most fields seems to shun, if not to abhor, formalism of any kind but more especially symmetry. If that actually is true and not simply a subjective reaction, then organ case design does not follow the general trend for only one in seven of the cases illustrated is asymmetrical. If one were to throw in the scores of pseudo-cases and organ "fronts" which come off the assembly lines each year, the ratio of asymmetrical to symmetrical compositions would fall much lower.

In small organs, the form of the asymmetrical case often merely follows the arrangement of the pipes upon the chest as in the Kuhn organ (96) in Baden, Switzerland, the Schantz (96) in Kent, Ohio, and the Hauptwerk of the Sipe-Yarbrough (86) in Mesquite, Texas, all of which have chromatic chests, or the Rückpositiv of the Flentrop (96) in Alabama College, Montevallo, and the Hauptwerk of the Schmid (37) in Bad Kohlgrub, Germany, which have N-chests.

The Klais case in St. Dionysius in Monheim-Baumberg (83) is a simple rectangular parallelepiped composed of three rectangular parallelepipeds; the relationship of the three division façades to one another and to the whole looks as if it might have been derived by the rules of dynamic symmetry developed by Jay Hambidge.

It takes a daring designer to essay asymmetry on the major axis of a building; just such a feat has been accomplished in the Rieger organ in the Archiepiscopal Seminary (83) in Cologne. Its success results from the excellent balance about the vertical axis. This work of Josef von Glatter-Götz is somewhat reminiscent of his earlier design in the Pfarrkirche St. Peter in Beuel-Vilich.[37]

At first glance the Klais cases (85) in St. Stephanus-Münster in Breisach and the Propstei St. Peter in Merzig, Saar, appear to be similar but the similarity lies only in the corresponding placement of each of the four divisions. A careful study of the two will show how different in detail they are. Each open division of each organ is asymmetrical within itself, yet both organs have excellent architectural balance.

The Klais organ in St. Maria in den Benden (84) in Düsseldorf-Wersten is in an alcove quite disoriented from the functional plan of the church; this explains the open ends of the Hauptwerk and Oberwerk cases for the open corners point toward the altar. The designer

---

[37] Illustrated in John Fesperman: *The Organ as Musical Medium* (Coleman-Ross Co., Inc., New York, 1962).

of the three cases for the same builder's organ in the Regina Marty-rum (84), a church in Berlin-Plötzensee built as a memorial to political prisoners of World War II, has achieved asymmetry in as imaginative a way as the designer of the Flentrop case in Malmö (59) retained symmetry. In Malmö, balanced voids above the pipes were attained in a symmetrical case by adjusting the lengths of the Prestant feet. Here the feet lengths are symmetrical about the vertical axis and the voids are balanced by letting the case tops follow the Prestant tops. Not only has the designer put curves in the case tops for added interest but he has reversed the C and C-sharp sides between Rückpositiv and Hauptwerk cases to give balance to the masses and silhouettes.

A unique case is that of the Marcussen organ in the Vor Frue Kirke (71) in Vordingborg. Here the Hauptwerk and Pedal divisions are on common C-chests and C-sharp chests in towers symmetrical about the vertical axis. The asymmetry is introduced by the two divisions in the center with their shuttered case following the chromatic arrangement of the chests. These are a Positiv opening to the front and another Positiv directly behind it which opens to the back.

The Marcussen organ in Sct. Nicolai Kirke in Aabenraa (62) and the one by Casavant Frères in the Church of St. Pascal in St. Pascal, Quebec (63), are examples of instruments having a single detached pedal tower. Another example is the van Vulpen organ of 1958 in the Opstandingskerk in Eindhoven.[18] When the pedal is on a single chest, it is more common to have its case a part of the whole as in the four organs illustrated on pages 86 and 87, or attached to the Hauptwerk case as in the Baden and Montevallo organs illustrated on page 96.

Such features as the heavy impost brackets with reverse curves, perhaps inspired by the old case in Garding, Germany,[4] of the St. Pascal case (63) and the long levers, possibly inspired by the little Frobenius organ[4] in the Frederiksberg Hospital in Copenhagen, for operating the sliders of the Sipe-Yarbrough organ in St. Stephen, Mesquite (86), are felicitous ideas for giving added interest and individuality to the case designs.

ENGLISH CASES

To search for contemporary cases in England is disheartening for, if it is possible, England is farther behind Teutonic Europe than is the United States. Although it is excellent in design, the most outstanding case in that country, that for a part of the enlargement of the organ in Bradford Cathedral, cannot be compared with the modern European casework because it is in the tradition of the great centrally located organs of English cathedrals. (The Church of St. Peter in Bradford was made a cathedral about a decade ago.) The Hill, Norman & Beard nave organ (77), playable from the console of a large organ of five divisions as well as from its own portable keyboard, stands over the center aisle toward the rear of the nave.

The case is bold, elegant and architectonic. Its effectiveness results from its studied proportions and from the simplicity of its elements: the plain cushion capitals (similar to some of the Norman capitals in Durham Cathedral) of its supporting columns, the severe raking base, and the unadorned pilasters which carry the center arch and the flying hoods over the corner pipe towers. Aside from the modest crosses on capitals and base, the only applied ornamentation, the cross and orb and the bishop's arms flanked by the kneeling angels, is as robust in character as the rest of the case. I do not know the actual colors, but can imagine gold on the cross and orb and red, blue, gold and perhaps silver on the arms. The Prestants are of bright spotted metal. Permitting the mitre to obscure the pipe mouths and forcing some pipe lengths are the only questionable features. The camber of the platform at the bottom is good, and the Fanfare Trumpets at the top help to give this case a liveliness which in no way decreases the lofty dignity befitting a cathedral.

The illustrations include three other recent English organs: the Hill, Norman & Beard instrument in Kings Park Roman Catholic Church in Glasgow, Scotland (37), that of J. W. Walker & Sons Ltd. in the Church of St. John the Evangelist, Islington, London (90), and the one by N. P. Mander Ltd. in St. Philip's, Kensington, London (90).

These three are treated here mainly for documentary reasons for if they were on the European continent, they would be omitted. They are the best of what appears to be a breakthrough in English case design. They are the first gropings in the right direction. An excellent distinction which the three have in common is their rear gallery location. They also have in common a frugality of detail which, although not necessarily a virtue, is never a defect. Incidentally, not one of the four English organs in the illustrations has mechanical action.

The main case in St. John the Evangelist appears to be a variant of the Salamanca type but actually is not for the center tower is only in the façade. The Rückpositiv is a variation of the Totentanz type. The curving lines of the pipe mouths are in the tradition of the English cases of the Georgian period.

It should be obvious to the observer that what is seen of the organ in St. Philip's is not an organ case but rather a façade and so, strictly speaking, is not within my subject. It is illustrated because it is quite possibly a major step toward unequivocal contemporary cases in England. In the light of the English predilection for pipes of false length, the Prestants of this organ are indeed refreshing. The designer further shows his freedom by balancing reeds with Prestants. Not only is the organ the design of Noel Mander but also the gallery which is carried forward within the nave arcades.

The lack of progress of modern English case design is even less understandable than that of the United States. Where we are remote from Europe, they are in close proximity to the countries which are producing a wealth of fresh and stimulating designs. Where our heritage of pre-Victorian cases is limited to a sprinkling of Georgian Colonial examples along the Atlantic seaboard, the English have a rich tradition ranging from the famous cases[4] in Old Radnor, Stanford-on-Avon and Tewkesbury, all of which are still in existence, down through the numerous Georgian organs.

VICTIMS OF ARCHITECTURE

ᐒᕈᕲ

The organ builder is often the victim of the architecture of the building. His most frequently encountered problem resulting from the architectural environment in which he must work is that of bad acoustics but that in itself is a problem of sound rather than vision and is not within my subject. His next most frequent architectural problem is that of the low ceiling.

Low ceilings are to be expected in residences and practice rooms and the builder can adapt small organs to these spaces without great difficulty. The Frels organ in the Brooks residence (79) in Sulphur, Louisiana, the Flentrop organs (96) in Salem College and Alabama College, the Kuhn organ in the Methodist Church in Baden, Switzerland (96), and the Schantz in Kent State University (96) are examples.

In St. Stephen Methodist Church[38] in Mesquite (86), the Sipe-Yarbrough case takes advantage of nearly all of the available height and the ceiled gable of the Reformed Church in Hüttwilen, Switzerland (87), has dictated the form of the Kuhn organ case. In the chapel of St. Joseph's Hospital (93) in Burgbrohl, the designer of the Klais organ has raised it as high as the ceiling would allow; this is true also of the Delaware organ in Our Lady of Mount Carmel (39) in Yonkers.

When a builder must place a rather large organ in a gallery having a relatively low ceiling, the only thing he can do is to spread the organ horizontally. An interesting off-axis solution to this problem is that of the Klais organ in the chapel of St. Catherine's Hospital (95) in Frankfurt. A larger organ, the Schmid in St. Bartholomew's Church (93) in Nürnberg, emphasizes verticality with the heavy intermediate members in the three case façades. The feeling of height is further accentuated by the highly attenuated feet of the treble Prestants in the Rückpositiv. Another way to emphasize height in this situation is to locate the Pedal division in two detached towers and to divide each division façade into strong vertical compartments with the pipes arranged in systems of alternates. This is the best treatment for on-axis symmetrical compositions; two successful examples are the Klais organ in St. Jacobi (92) in Schutterwald, Germany, and the Casavant organ in the United Lutheran Church (94), Grand Forks, North Dakota. As mentioned elsewhere, the Klais organ has a system of double and triple bialternates; the Casavant has quadruple

---

[38] The room in which this organ stands is a temporary sanctuary; it was designed for other purposes after the permanent sanctuary is built.

alternates throughout. It will be seen that both these organs take full advantage of the ceiling height. The Casavant organ gives interest to the rear of an interior which otherwise has little to distinguish it from a school auditorium.

When a new organ is to go into a building built a generation or two ago and which has organ chambers, the designer should not let such a situation intimidate him. There are a number of buildings today with rear-gallery installations which originally had chambered organs at the front. One is Unity Church in St. Paul which now has a Noack mechanical-action organ (91) in a rear gallery. This building was gutted by fire; the architects for the remodelling, Hammel & Green, provided a gallery as striking as that in the Pauluskerk (44) in The Hague. Sometimes church committees can be persuaded that they do not have to have exactly what they had before.

Often a new organ must be designed for an old building which, to say the least, is not an enhancing environment for it. The center case of the Delaware organ (37) in the Church of the Assumption in Tuckahoe, New York, is a definite improvement over its architectural environment; its designer not only had a rather low ceiling to contend with but he also kept the round window unobscured. The other divisions of the organ which stand at each end of the balcony are less satisfactory because they have been influenced too much by the architecture of the building.[39]

The church in Egg, Austria, which houses a new Rieger organ (91) is quite undistinguished architecturally; here the unadorned case is much better than its environment. This organ is unusual in that the cases on the rail house a divided Hauptwerk with a Prestant 8′; the case above the Swell at the rear is the Pedal showing a Prestant 16′.[40] A detached console, just back of the gallery rail, is placed so that the organist faces the choir with his back to the altar. To the benefit of the casework, a new section of railing of modern design has been set between the forward cases, serving the same purpose as those in Nieuwendijk (48).

[39] These were purposely cropped from the photograph because I felt they detracted from a commendable effort.
[40] This is how I remember it after a year. I made no written notes as I thought I would obtain additional information from Mr. von Glatter-Götz; as my memory is sometimes faulty, there may be error in these statements.

ACTIONS IN CASES

꿍

It may be assumed that all the European and Canadian organs in the illustrations which are designated as having mechanical key action also have slider chests with the sliders operated either manually or electrically. This is not true of all the mechanical-action organs built in the United States; some of these have mechanico-pneumatic or electro-pneumatic stop actions on barred chests.

Some American builders seem to hold the belief that organs with any of the available electro-pneumatic or direct-electric chests cannot be placed in cases. It is true that most of them require more space than barred chests but it is not a prohibitive excess. The Casavant in the Basilique Notre-Dame-du-Cap in Cap-de-la-Madeleine, Quebec (65), and the Aeolian-Skinner in the Alice Millar Chapel[41] in Evanston, Illinois (75), are large electro-pneumatic instruments in cases. Five church organs of moderate size with electric action are the Gress-Miles instruments (36) in Woodlawn and Spring Valley, New York, and Portland, Oregon, the Van Zoeren, Henderson and Steinkampf organ in Stamford, Connecticut (38), and the Delaware Organ Company's in Yonkers, New York (39). The Frels in Sulphur, Lousiana (79), and the Schantz in Kent, Ohio (96), are examples of small electric-action organs in cases.

[41] At Northwestern University's Conference on Church Music, April, 1964, during a panel discussion in the rear gallery of the Alice Millar Chapel, I made the remark that I thought the fact that one of the big U.S. companies had at last built an organ in a case was a major breakthrough in organ building in this country. I was mistaken for time has proven that this case was no more than a sport. Later, I learned that the case was there only at the insistence of Grigg Fountain, University organist and choirmaster, to obtain "organized divisional organ sound" (one of the tenets of the *Werkprinzip*).

EPILOGUE

〜

Although most of the major companies of American continue to build obsolete organs, we are nevertheless in a golden age of organ building. The resurgence which began, developed and flowered in the Germanic countries of Europe, is now making impact in the United States. The situation here is similar to that of twenty years ago in Europe.

It is the revival of the organ case, a corollary of the resurgence, which will compel American church architects to revolutionize their approach to church design. They will be forced to consider acoustics, ceiling heights and location of choir and organ with increased seriousness. Instead of evading the problem by merely providing a place for amplifiers for some electronic device or screening off a space for an obsolete type of pipe organ, they will be obliged to recognize the organ as a functional instrument in the worship service requiring a case worthy of the architect's consideration. They, along with American organ builders and church building committees, must come to realize that the cost of the organ case can be offset by the saving gained in eliminating the spaces and excess ranks of pipes required in current practices.

No period in the history of architecture surpasses in quality and imagination the total contemporary case design represented in the illustrations. It is abundant and exciting.

INDEX

Only the cities in which organs are located are indexed unless
more than one instrument in a particular location is mentioned
and then each building is indexed under the name of the place

125

This book was produced by letterpress and photo-lithography by the Marvin D. Evans Company of Fort Worth, Texas. The paper is 80 pound Natural Strathmore Artlaid Text and 80 pound Warren's Cameo Brilliant Dull. The type used is 10 and 8 point Janson. The book was bound by H. V. Chapman & Sons of Abilene, Texas. Design and end papers are by the author.